High Performance Trading

35 Practical Strategies and Techniques to Enhance Your Trading Psychology and Performance

by Steve Ward

HARRIMAN HOUSE LTD

3A Penns Road
Petersfield
Hampshire
GU32 2EW
GREAT BRITAIN

Tel: +44 (0)1730 233870
Fax: +44 (0)1730 233880
Email: enquiries@harriman-house.com
Website: www.harriman-house.com

First published in Great Britain in 2009 by Harriman House.
Reprinted 2010

978-1-905641-61-1

British Library Cataloguing in Publication Data
A CIP catalogue record for this book can be obtained from the British Library.

Printed and bound in Great Britain by CPI Antony Rowe, Chippenham

To Sabine and Ollie

Contents

Part Three – Evaluation, Analysis and Improving and Sustaining Performance 201

About the Author

Steve Ward is a performance consultant, trader performance coach, director of High Performance Trading and has traded FX and stock indices. He provides specialised trader performance and psychology coaching and training programmes for traders in the retail, proprietary and institutional sectors, and provides consultancy to trading and financial institutions across the globe working in the areas of trader recruitment, selection, assessment, training and development. Steve has extensive experience as an in-house performance coach and trainer for leading trading institutions, and in co-managing a large team of over 40 professional traders in London. He was a consultant to the BBC TV series *Million Dollar Traders* and is a regular trainer at the London Stock Exchange.

Steve has a history of working with elite level performers including athletes and sports teams at world championship and Olympic level. His work utilises techniques and strategies from sports and performance psychology, cognitive behavioural and performance coaching, and behavioural finance, to help traders to develop the success skills and winning mindset required to achieve their trading goals.

High Performance Trading

High Performance Trading is a leading supplier of trading psychology and performance services to traders and trading institutions across the globe.

We work with traders, helping them to achieve and sustain high performance, to develop the skills and winning mindset required, thereby maximising their trading potential and profitability.

We offer our clients a wide range of high quality services and products including:

- 1:1 trader psychology and performance coaching

- Seminars and workshops

- Online High Performance Trading training programme

- High Performance Trading weekend seminars

- Resources, including books and articles

- Consultancy services in recruiting, selecting, training and developing traders

If you would like to find out more about how to enhance your trading performance and maximise your profitability, do pay a visit to our website or email direct.

www.highperformancetrading.co.uk

info@highperformancetrading.co.uk

Acknowledgements

There have of course been many people who have been instrumental in helping and guiding me to be where I am today and who have helped me to achieve many of my goals and ambitions (this book being one of them!) and so I would like to take this opportunity to say a few heartfelt thank yous.

The Oscars read as follows!

For their lifelong support and encouragement – my parents Vic and Judy Ward.

For supporting me in pursuing the things I love to do – my beautiful wife Sabine and my amazing son and champion Oliver.

For always being there when needed – my lifelong best mate Blairy.

For his wisdom and encouragement – a great coach and ever-improving Yoda impersonator, Donald MacNaughton.

For igniting my passion for performance psychology and setting me loose in the world of sports psychology – Jeffrey Hodges.

For setting me on the path to trading psychology – Gavin Gobby.

For introducing me to the institutional world of trading – Khoi Tu.

For teaching me to trade and introducing me to the world of retail trading – Nick McDonald.

For some great business ideas and some great times together over the years – David Helps and Delme Thompson.

For the opportunity to work at 'probably' the best proprietary trading group in the world and for supporting me in the writing of this book – Sonny Schneider and Matthew Silvester

For making this book possible – every trader I have ever worked with; everyone who has given input and feedback; and also to the many authors who have led the field in trading psychology, and provided inspiration to my own study of this topic, most notably Brett Steenbarger, Mark Douglas and Ari Kiev.

And finally to the most understanding editorial team in the world – we got there!

Thank you all.

Preface

It was 2005 when I first entered the world of trading, having previously spent my time working in sports and performance psychology with elite athletes, sports teams and corporate clients. I was invited to London to present some seminars on performance psychology to a large trading institution, with an audience comprised of about 150 traders. I was initially disappointed to find that not one of them wore a pinstripe suit or bowler hat and that the dress code seemed more akin to mandatory jeans and t-shirts. It was, however, the beginning of what has been an amazing journey of learning and discovery, in which I have become ever more involved in the world of financial trading, even becoming a trader myself.

The premise behind my initial invitation was simple but novel. The institution had been looking to create the very best environment to train successful traders in, and which the best traders would want to work from, too. But something was still missing.

They had a fantastic modern office right in the heart of the City; they provided the best trading platforms and charting packages; they had developed an excellent graduate training programme; they had high speed connectivity, impressive risk management and just about everything that a trader could want. (Including a games room and a concierge service!) Yet they felt that the performance of the traders could still be better – and ultimately after having looked at all of the possible environmental and external factors that contribute to trading success, they finally looked to the most important person in the trading equation: the trader himself. Enabling the trader to perform at his or her peak for as much of the time as possible was seen as being key to maximising the profitability of the individual and therefore the organisation.

> **The trader performing at their peak for as much of the time as possible is key to maximising profitability.**

Over a period of almost twelve months I presented regular seminars to the traders on topics such as emotional state management, goal achievement, concentration and focussing, the development of a trader's mindset – as well as working with many traders on a 1:1 and group coaching basis. The feedback was exceptionally positive, and from this beginning I ended up working with institutions and traders across the globe, embarking on a path that I had never envisioned but am now absolutely passionate about. Why?

The world of trading is dynamic, results-driven and highly pressurised: all of the factors that I had enjoyed so much in working alongside the sporting world. Yet trading for me offered something different, too – it was a much more complex and demanding puzzle. Trading has so many components to it that can influence performance. The markets are an ever-evolving and truly dynamic environment. Traders expect demonstrable results, and always demand the highest level of performance from themselves. So here within trading was almost a greater, more intricate challenge: how to bolster, refine and constantly improve the performance, not of physical athletes, but of participants in complex global finance. To this day I am of course still learning so much from working with traders, trader managers, trainers and other coaches, and there is always new research to be read and considered. But you hold in your hands the distillation of the wisdom and experience I have accrued so far, in this rigorous and enjoyable process.

The pursuit of my passion for high-performance in trading is something that I feel fortunate to be able to undertake each and every day. I have also become a trader myself, and so have, in many ways, become the athlete as well as the coach! Each time I trade is a reminder for me of the demands and joys involved in becoming a successful trader.

Steve Ward, 2009

Introduction

This book is entitled *High Performance Trading* and is a practical guide to enhancing your trading performance and psychology. It is about helping you to achieve and then, most importantly, sustain high performance.

The book is divided into three core parts, representing the three areas of the 'performance cycle' – planning and preparation; execution; and evaluation and analysis leading into performance improvement.

Trading performance and the results that it brings are the hub of the trading performance and psychology wheel. The three dimensions are the core components to achieving success, not just in trading but in any performance activity.

In Part One, 'Planning and Preparing for Trading Success', we look at how we can set ourselves up for trading success and what we can do to stack the odds of success in our favour.

In Part Two, 'Decision-Making, Discipline and Flawless Execution', we look at practical approaches for making more effective trading decisions, improving your trading discipline and for adopting a flawless execution approach.

In Part Three, 'Evaluation, Analysis and Improving and Sustaining Performance', we explore how to measure and assess trading performance so that we can get the valuable feedback required to help us to identify what we should do more of, what we should do less of, what we should start doing, and what we should stop doing. Importantly, we then look at how to improve performance, how to change behaviour – and how to become a better trader.

High-performance trading is more than a set of techniques and strategies, though; it is an approach, a mindset, a philosophy. A high-performance approach is founded on the desire, passion and commitment to achieve the best possible standard of performance: by putting in the effort and time to develop the required skills, knowledge and understanding; by accepting responsibility for your results, and understanding that at any given time the results you are getting are purely a reflection of your current performance level, your ability, knowledge and skills.

As Brett Steenbarger notes in *Enhancing Trading Performance*, "When a person truly commits to achieving excellence in an area, and becomes absorbed in the process of achieving their best possible performance, they will automatically begin to make changes to their outlook, perception and beliefs, and to adopt performance orientated behaviours."

The high-performance approach to trading is typified by the following:

- Striving to be the best trader that you can be – focussing on personal excellence – and working on achieving and sustaining the highest levels of performance possible, underpinned by strong motivation and commitment.

- Setting yourself up for success through the development of goals, a trading strategy, a business approach, and training and practice.

- Focussing on the flawless execution of your strategy, making the best possible decisions and staying disciplined. Evaluating and analysing performance regularly and using this feedback to make the required changes to enhance your trading performance.

- Persisting during the good and the bad times.

High Performance Trading is the result of over five years spent working full-time with financial traders across the globe in institutions and proprietary trading groups, and with retail trading clients in the arena of trading performance and psychology. It is intended to be a sharing of ideas, findings and thoughts that have been drawn from my experience of trader recruitment, selection, assessment, development, training and coaching with traders of all ages, experiences, success levels and asset classes. I have also drawn on the knowledge and expertise of the traders

> **❝** This is a user manual of practical and useful approaches, strategies and techniques that you can implement right away. **❞**

that I have had the pleasure of working with, the industry leaders in the world of trader training and coaching, as well as the many excellent books that exist on performance, sports psychology, personal development and trading psychology.

The intention behind this book is not to provide a theoretical discussion of leading topics in trading psychology (as there are many good ones already in existence). Rather, it is to provide a user manual of practical and useful approaches, strategies and techniques that you can implement within your own trading to enhance your current level of performance. Not every strategy or technique will be relevant for everyone and indeed I hope that this book will be used equally as a reference book, dipped in and out of, and picked up and read as and when circumstances dictate – from my own reading I know that what I see as valuable in a book is most often dictated by where I am at with my performance myself.

Before I started to put this book together I asked traders what they wanted from a book on trading performance and psychology, and here are the key items they suggested:

- Practical strategies and techniques

- Easy to read and access information

- Short chapters

- Diagrams

- Stories and case studies to illustrate points

I have aimed to write this book for you, the trader, following the formula that traders suggested, and covering the topics that they felt would be most useful. In essence this is a book by the trader and for the trader. My greatest hope is that you get something useful and valuable from these pages, that you take the time and effort to apply such lessons, and that your trading performance is enhanced as a result.

If you have the urge for greater in-depth knowledge or a more theoretical understanding of some of these areas then I would refer you to the recommended texts and resources listed throughout the book and also in the appendix.

My own personal measure of success for this book will be the number of people that took something from it, implemented into their trading and experienced a positive improvement in performance – let me know if that was you!

Part One

Planning and Preparing for Trading Success

STRATEGY 1

Set Yourself Up for Success

"Becoming a great trader is a marathon not a sprint!"

– Abe Cohen, trader mentor

Transforming into a Trade

In my consulting role with traders
with professional proprietary trad
different points along the learnii
traders I work with I have known for severai ye..
some of them grow from being excited trainee beginners to consist..
profitable professionals. The traders who become successful and profitable have
achieved something that most people who take up trading do not – they have
become traders. What do I mean by this? They have transformed from *learning*
to trade, through *becoming* traders, to *being* traders. Each phase has its own
distinct make-up, and transition from one to another is a process that takes
place over time.

Here are a few thoughts on what may differentiate a trader at different phases
of this transformational process:

Transformational trading – 3 stages to becoming a trader

1. Learning to Trade

- Develop required basic skills, knowledge and understanding.

- Spend time on simulators/paper trading, practicing basics.

- Trading small size in live markets.

- Developing key actions and disciplines.

- Working from directed knowledge – perhaps trading a strategy learnt from
  a course.

- Focus on developing basic trading skills.

- Conscious execution of skills – moving from incompetence to competence.

- May still be naive about the challenge and difficulty of achieving trading
  success.

- Prone to overconfidence from early successes in the market.

personalize their trading strategy and style.

development of skills, knowledge and understanding.

s on developing trading competence.

ome skills becoming more subconscious through repetition and practice.

- Likely to have encountered periods of drawdown and losses that have tested their commitment, self-belief and resilience.

- Developing awareness of importance of psychology and performance in trading.

3. Trader

- Has the skill and ability to develop and execute strategy in line with own abilities, skill and strengths, as well as preferred risk, decision-making, information-processing and behavioural styles.

- Extensive levels of unconscious competence.

- Continual improvement is still a focus.

- Focus on developing trading expertise and mastery.

- Flexible and adaptable to changing market and personal circumstances.

- Able, if prepared and willing, to coach and mentor traders.

- Experienced – 'weathered' – in the markets!

- Fully understands the importance of psychology in achieving consistent trading performance.

- Less focussed on P&L and more focussed on execution and mastering their craft.

Although I have given three discrete categories here, we are really looking at a continuum of development as shown in the following diagram.

12-4 Every Day Trading Hours

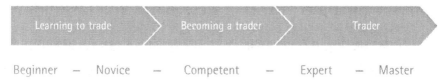

Beginner — Novice — Competent — Expert — Master

Where would you place yourself on this continuum?

What is the evidence for that?

Time Precedes Success

Devotion Devotion Devotion

"Only time determines whether you will become a successful trader."

– Harold Cataquet, trader coach, Cataquet Associates

In my younger days I was a keen martial artist studying both Aikdo and Jiu Jitsu. I remember one day asking my sensei (teacher) what he felt the most important quality or distinguishing factor was between those students who achieved black belt, and those that didn't. "That is easy," he said, "the people who make black belt just keep coming and training hard."

In essence the key success factor was time: keeping engaged in the activity long enough to get good at it. Time is actually a big factor in achieving success in all high-performance arenas; and trading is no exception. In his book *Outliers*, which examines what it takes to become highly successful in any given area, Malcolm Gladwell gives the figure of of 10,000 hours' commitment. In *The Road to Excellence*, K. Anders Ericsson estimates ten years; and there is of course the old adage that 'it takes ten years to become an overnight success'. One of my favourite ways of putting this basic demand for commitment comes from Steve Lumley, a UK triathlon coach, talking about how long it takes to reach peak level performance in elite triathlon competition – 4 x 6 x 48 x 10. (Or 4 hours a day for 6 days each week, for 48 weeks of the year, for 10 years.)

Over the years I have been very fortunate to see many traders make the transition from beginner, to novice, to competent, to expert trader; achieving high levels of success and reaping the return on the significant amounts of time, energy and in some cases money that they have invested early on in their careers. The one common factor in all of their cases is that they spent long enough in the markets to develop the required levels of skill, knowledge, attitudes and behaviours. Success was not achieved overnight. They survived the learning curve and got to the earning curve! Many people, on the other hand, drop out through running out of personal or trading capital, not being resilient enough to cope with the stress and pressure of trading, or through frustration at the difficulty of the challenge that trading presents.

Getting to When it Clicks

Time enables you to not only acquire the skills, knowledge, attitudes and behaviours that are required to trade successfully but it also keeps you in the game so that you can get to the 'clicking point'.

One of the most fundamental obstacles that you must overcome as a trader is the task of ensuring that you stay in the markets for as long as is possible until it has clicked – and then you are off!

ALWAYS STAY LONG ENUF IN THE MARKET UNTIL RESULT IS ACHIEVE.

Real Life Examples: Getting to the Clicking Point

"I believe that every new trader is working towards that day when things 'click'. It obviously happens at different speeds for different people. The key thing is to keep yourself in the markets long enough to allow it to happen for you.

"I had been struggling to get my trading account up through a certain level and achieve what I felt was the next step in my trading career. I was doing the right things and trading well, but every time my account got near to this financial level, things started to go a little wrong. I felt confident in what I was doing as I was being fairly consistent and diligent in my approach. I spoke to a much more senior trader about this and he advised me to remain patient. He said if I kept doing the right things then the opportunities would come; I should seize them when they did.

"Pretty basic advice, but just what I needed to hear. Soon afterwards an opportunity did arrive, and because I was confident and focussed I capitalised well and burst through that barrier. From there I've never really looked back. Maintaining the right practices and keeping my discipline allowed me to stay solvent and in the markets long enough for a big opportunity to come along. Having a good strategy and plan allowed me to recognise and capitalise on that opportunity."

– Stewart Hampton, Trader

"I remember the day it all clicked. I remember it so clearly. To this day I am still not sure why it did – but it did! Interestingly, when it clicks, all the stuff everyone said was important, but you thought was too easy to be significant, realises itself."

– Nick McDonald, Trade With Precision

Experience Counts

Experience is one of the most important factors behind consistently successful traders, and experience is purely an outcome of time. What happens over this period that is so critical?

- Learning from mistakes

- Improved knowledge, skills and understanding

- Improved knowledge of self and strengths/weaknesses

- Pattern recognition

- Experience different market conditions

- Conditioning of behaviours and responses

For every trader, getting to the stage where you have acquired sufficient market time and gained the required level of competence is a primary goal. How long is this period? How long is a piece of string! It will be different for different people. We are all unique, with our own particular set of circumstances. We are, however, talking years here – and not days. This is a serious endeavour, as all truly profitable pursuits must be.

"How long does it take to know that you are a successful trader? This is a difficult question. A good friend of mine who is involved with business development suggests that once you have got past the first three years then you are probably quite established, so it may be something similar for a trader."

– Nick Shannon, occupational psychologist

The J-Curve

One of the most important strategies a trader can adopt is to do everything possible to make sure that they stay in the game long enough to get good at it and for it to click. This is what I call setting yourself up for real success –

> **" You have to learn to stay in the game long enough to get good at it. "**

putting in place specific actions and strategies to create enduring, rather than transitory, achievement.

When you learn to trade it is not uncommon to see performance shape itself as what is known as a J-Curve, as shown in the diagram below. The J-Curve is a typical and common development curve for traders. In the early stages of their career they are still learning, and so execution is not accurate or well refined – leading to perhaps more losses. There is also a greater chance of errors being made, and commissions and costs still have to be paid. This can lead to a typical dip in trading account balance whilst the trader is essentially trying to learn how to not lose money, how to manage risk and establish good trading habits. In phase two, the trader is now focussed on making money, is making less errors, and the execution of their strategy is improving. In the third phase the trader is at break-even – covering costs and losses with their trading. Finally the trader enters profitability. It is important to note that progression and growth is not ongoing or exponential from this point and that in fact some traders can go backwards quite significantly.

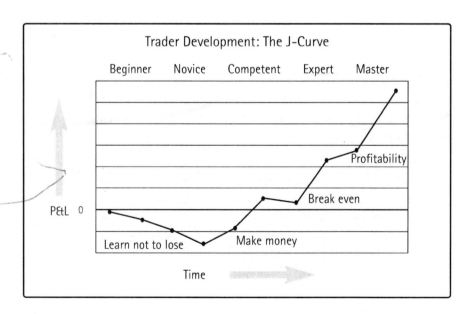

Trader Development: The J-Curve

Different traders will have different devel[...]
on many factors, including the products [...]
commission structures, any overheads, [...]
accelerators can be utilised to sustain pro[...]

For some traders, growth occurs from earl[...]
time. For others there is a long phase of [...]

Beliefs, attitu[...]
success an[...]

Devel[...]
ex[...]

•   •   •

Short and Shallow – Tradir[...]

For all traders, keeping the dip in the curve as short and as shallow as possible is the key to enhancing your profitability and becoming successful as a trader. With this in mind, it is important to understand that there are specific factors that enable this to happen, and that you can actively implement these factors to accelerate and sustain your progress along the curve – I call them the Trading Success Factors.

For example, poor risk and money management can have a big impact on the depth to which the J-Curve goes. Likewise, the amount of time that you can actively spend trading the markets, and the quality of the training and coaching that you get, can have a significant impact on how long it takes to break even.

Practical Strategy: Trading Success Factors

Take a look at the list below of Trading Success Factors. Which do you have already? Are there areas where you could develop and enhance your performance? What do you need to work on and develop next in order to continue developing your trading?

- Strength of purpose and commitment – critical to keep you going
- Resilience – psychological/physical/financial
- Strong risk and money management strategies
- Training, coaching and mentoring – high quality, organised and structured
- Ability to learn and adapt
- Skills, knowledge, understanding
- Hard work and effort

…es, perceptions about yourself, trading, the markets, … money/wealth

…pment of a suitable and successful strategy with an edge/positive …ectancy

Timing of entry to the markets – is the current market conducive to learning

- Love of trading and the markets
- Time/immersion – time to learn and trade
- Support – friends, family, colleagues
- Deliberate, focussed practice

 Trader Top Tips

"A good friend of mine always told me to make sure that you live to fight another day. That was invaluable advice."

– David Helps, LIFFE

"Manage your risk, it will give you the staying power to succeed."

– SJG, trader

"In order to become a successful trader I believe that the key thing is hard work. When you begin you must immerse yourself fully in every single aspect of the job. You can never know too much."

– Lawrie Inman, trader

"Personally I feel success requires similar core traits and commitments, independent of the occupation. It is simply magnified in trading, because an individual's survival does not rest in the hands of an employer, and perhaps more so, because our decisions yield rapid results, be them favourable or otherwise.

"With this in mind, I would advise traders that resilience, money management and emotional control are, in my experience, essential in achieving long-term success. I am firmly of the belief that at the opening stages of a trading career, it is not the technical know-how that most separates the level of achievement of the individual, but his/her ability to apply their plans in real time, and it is the above mentioned attributes the facilitate that."

– Edward Arees, trader

"Be first in the office, take no holidays for the first two years, and get to know the best traders around you."

– Mark Lindop, trader

"In the beginning your aim should be to develop confidence and structure. Get comfortable with your trading strategy, develop good habits and discipline and be prepared to do whatever it takes to achieve success. It is critical that you avoid getting yourself into a situation where you are desperate and have to make money – this is the situation that more than any other seems to have the most destructive effect on a person and their ability to trade well."

– Matthew Silvester, head of training, Schneider Trading Associates

STRATEGY 2

It's Down to You – Taking Responsibility for Your Performance

"You are the most important variable in the trading equation."

– Mike Elvin, Financial Risk Taking

Who is to Blame?

Think back to a time when you had a losing trade, or made an error with your trade execution, or had a bad trading day. Who or what was responsible for the result that you got? The market? The broker? The trading platform you were using? The room you were in? The weather?

One of the most important factors in becoming a high-performing trader and achieving and sustaining trading success – and perhaps the core principle of this book – is that *you* are responsible for your trading results. The results that you get in your trading are created by *you*.

Read this...

> *"I am responsible for my trading results. I accept that I create my trading experience."*

How did that feel? Think back to your trading – has this been true for you? Have you taken responsibility for your results or have you looked to find someone or something to blame?

> "Everything may be taken from us except the last of the human freedoms –
> our ability to choose our own attitudes in every situation."
>
> **– Victor E. Frankyl, Man's Search for Meaning**

It is not an easy concept to take on board. However, understanding that the level of your trading success and the results you get is absolutely under your control, is fundamental to becoming a high-performance trader, and achieving high levels of consistent success. It is easy to find some other cause for our poor performance; to create stories that shift the focus away from ourselves and onto external factors. In doing this though we take ourselves out of the learning and development loop. By not taking responsibility for your actions you do not enable yourself to reflect on what you did and what you could do differently next time. Instead you are left to wait for external factors to change to get you the results you want – you have disempowered yourself and given control of your trading results to external factors. You are drifting on the waves of the market, with no rudder!

The Personal Responsibility Formula

Jack Canfield in *The Success Principles* introduces this formula for taking responsibility:

E + R = O

(Event + Response = Outcome)

The basic premise of the formula is that you cannot control the events that happen, but the outcome that you get from such events is then governed by how you respond to them.

In trading terms I have adapted this formula to the following:

M + T = P&L

(Market + Trader = Profit and Loss)

Your trading results are an outcome of how the market trades and how you trade the markets. Which do we have greater control of? How we trade the markets.

> "The one thing you can control is you."
>
> **– Mark Douglas, *The Disciplined Trader***

If you do not like the results that you are getting in your trading then there are essentially two paths that you can take:

1. You can blame the markets (and within this side of the equation I would also include brokers, etc) for your P&L. This is the easiest of the two options and I am not saying that market conditions are not a factor, or else they would not be in the equation at all. However, what we should consider is that they are not the *deciding* factor.

2. You can look at how you traded the market, and therefore how you created your P&L. This is the hardest of the two! What you are doing here, though, is taking responsibility for your P&L. You are accepting that you have created the outcome by trading in the way that you have. If you are unhappy with your results then you need to look at how you can change your trading performance until you get the results that you want. You might need to change your thinking, your perception or beliefs, your mental processes, your trading strategy and ultimately your trading behaviours. Your trading

behaviour is what you have control of – and this governs your trading performance. For more experienced traders any existing unhelpful behaviours will be largely conditioned and habitual and this can present a slightly greater challenge in making the required behaviour changes.

How Have You Created Your Results?

"Strategies don't make money – people do. I have taught the same strategy to thousands of people, all of whom have achieved different levels of success – they did the same course in the same room with the same person and some of them at the same time. What is the difference? The person!"

– Nick McDonald, Trade With Precision

Taking responsibility for your trading results and asking yourself "How did I create that?" is a powerful way of ensuring that you enter a learning loop that will move your trading performance forward. If you do not take this approach, then ultimately you are leaving yourself to drift at the hands of the market and you remain stuck. We get a demonstration of the old maxim: "If you keep on doing what you have always done, then you will keep on getting the results that you have always got."

When you look at your trading results and ask, "How did I create that result?" then you are in charge of the process. And if you don't like the result, you can start to look at what you did and what you will do differently in the future. And when you find the key actions/events that really produced your results, then you can make changes and get improved results.

Do you like the results you are producing as a trader?

If not, then how are you creating them and what do you need to do differently?

Practical Strategy: Taking Responsibility Through Powerful Questions

If you get a trading result or performance that was not what you wanted, then utilise the following powerful questions. Doing so will help you to take responsibility for your performance, enable you to get value from a bad experience and move on to becoming a better trader.

- How did I create that?

- What was my behaviour that led to that outcome?

- What was I thinking and feeling?

- What do I need to do differently to get the result I want next time?

STRATEGY 3

Fuelling Success – Motivation and Commitment

"There is no high level performance without purpose."

– A. Mulliner

Motivation is a Key Ingredient in Success

Having a strong motivation and purpose is a very important ingredient in achieving and, maybe more importantly, sustaining trading success. To achieve trading success we need three elements in place:

1. A strong interest in and commitment to trading (motivation, purpose, captivation, interest).

2. The desire to reach a high level of performance and understanding of what it will take to achieve that level (know your outcome and know the 'price' – what it will take to achieve the goal, which might include aspects such as time, effort, money and changes to lifestyle).

3. The willingness to put in the significant time and effort to reach that level (*paying* the price!)

(Adapted from *Human Performance: Cognition, Stress and Individual Differences*, 1985, 2000)

Motivation is therefore integral to achieving success. In very simple terms, it gives us the energy to *do* – to engage us and keep us engaged in the actions required to achieve

❝ Motivation is integral to success. It is the fuel for all the effort, adaptation and resilience required. ❞

requisite levels of knowledge and skill; to adopt the attitudes and behaviours that it takes to become a successful trader. Motivation is critical to achieving success as it fuels the ongoing action required. Strong motivation is also a component of resilience – the ability to bounce back from setbacks and to keep going in the face of adversity.

So what is motivation? Motives are reasons for doing. When we ask, "Why am I doing this?" or "What am I doing this for?" we are uncovering our motives. *Have you asked yourself that in your trading?* What was the situation? What was your answer? Ultimately, at some stage in a trader's career, they are going to be asking that question in relation to whether they should carry on trading or not. And the strength and power, or lack thereof, in their answers – their established level of motivation – may well be decisive in determining the outcome.

"If you want it you will do it, no matter what it takes!"

– Nigel Read, trader

Our strongest motivations are derived from our sense of purpose and our values (what is important to us). There is no high level performance without strong purpose!

Purpose is the foundation because strong motivation enables you to put in the significant and sustained effort required to achieve the skills, knowledge, attitudes and behaviour necessary to reach a high level of trading performance. It is the effort needed for effort.

Discovering Your Core Motivations

Here are some useful exercises to complete to help you to start to disccover and understand your core trading motivations, to begin to discover your purpose. It is really important that for each exercise you give yourself the time to complete them fully and that you do write your answers down.

Exercise: Values Elicitation

Take a few minutes and write down everything that is important to you in your life – family, friends, hobbies. Ask yourself, "What is important to me in life?"

Now rank them in order, the most important starting at 1.

Then consider how your life reflects your values. Are you living life in accordance with your values?

Where does trading fit in? How important is trading to you?

Exercise: Uncovering Your Core Trading Motivations

Why did you start trading? (Why do you want to trade? – if not actively trading)

What was it about trading that particularly attracted you?

What do you want from your trading? What would that give you?

What do you enjoy about trading? What do you not enjoy?

Why is trading/being a trader important to you?

Identifying Your Motivational Style

When we look at motivation, there are many theories and models that exist. One approach that I feel is particularly important for achieving high performance is having both positive motivation and intrinsic, or internal, motivation.

Positive motivation is when we move towards a desired outcome. Examples would include working hard for a bonus; following a healthy diet to feel good and have more energy. This is opposed to negative motivation, which is when we are prompted to act to *avoid* a consequence, e.g. working hard so that you do not get the sack!

Intrinsic or internal motivation is a motivation that comes from within. It is wanting to achieve a level of trading (or other) success because of the feeling you will get when you achieve that goal, not because of what anyone else will do. (External motivation, its opposite, is simply a motivation that comes from an external source, e.g. working hard to achieve praise or financial reward from another person; trying to prove someone wrong.)

Most motivations in life are a combination of two of these. Such a combination creates a motivation quadrant (see below). As you can see in Quadrant 1, we have a motivation that is positive and internal – achieving a self-set goal. Quadrant 2 is negative and internal – not wanting to fail yourself. Quadrant 3 is positive and external – working for a financial reward or bonus. Quadrant 4 is negative and external – doing a good job so that you do not get the sack.

It can be very interesting to assess your own trading motivations against these criteria.

Look back at your list of motivations that came out from the 'Uncovering Your Core Trading Motivations' exercise and for each one identify which quadrant it falls into. After you have completed this, look through the results – do you have a bias towards any particular quadrant(s)?

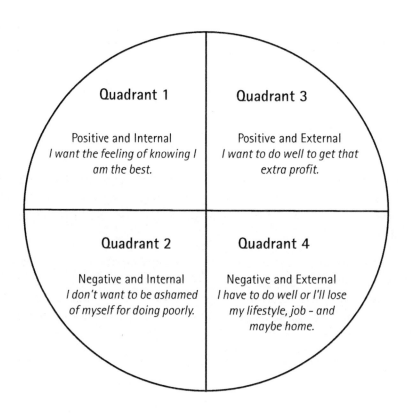

People often ask me which is the 'best' motivation style to use. The answer to this is that it is likely that most people will utilise more than one motivational style, and that, as with most attitudes, some flexibility is important in utilising them. Everyone is different, and nothing can be universally prescribed.

However, whatever the mix, I think it is important, as said, to get solid, positive internal motivation in there at some level. Performance psychologists have found that people are more successful when they stop focussing all of their energies on the outcome/results (which is interestingly one of the major causes behind performance anxiety), and learn to focus on just being excellent at the process of what they do. It is important to gain an understanding of the difference between doing things for a result, and doing something because you want to be good at it: focussing on the latter will often accomplish the former anyway, but it will not often work the other way round. Research has shown that it is this second, *internal*, motivation that ultimately sustains progress and performance, particularly when faced with challenges and difficulties. It is a key part of resilience.

As a trader, no doubt some of your motivations will be external (financial reward, recognition from others, material possessions), and this is quite proper. It is important to make sure, though, that any internal motivation is not superficial and dependent on the same things (e.g. just the buzz you get from trading, achieving a feeling of success). It must go deeper. As a trader, if you base *all* of your motivation – internal and external – around evanescent financial results, what will happen if you encounter a quieter period in the markets and your P&L gets lower? Or what will happen if you encounter a challenging time in your trading and your results are low? At the point where you most need your motivation and drive, they would actually be at their lowest. But people with strong internal motivation enjoy challenges, reversals and trials, as they know that this pushes them to be even better. For them, the old cliché is an inescapable fact: 'What doesn't kill you makes you stronger!'

Some Examples of Successful Trader Motivations

"Money and freedom; a long-term goal of having my own trading company; being my own boss; flexibility."

– **bond trader**

"Enjoying the game/winning; wealth and way of life; excitement and buzz; being my own boss; accountable to self; free time. All this in addition to a long-term vision of a nice house in the country, kids in private school, a lump sum in the bank, and still trading!"

– STIR trader

"Pitting my wits against the market; seeing things before others; staying calm under pressure; having responsibility for myself and my own actions; control; adrenaline rush; being my own boss."

– stock trader

Checking Your Motivations

As you start to uncover your motivations for wanting to be a successful trader, take time to analyse them. See whether, if you were to achieve success, it does in fact give you what you really want. Ed Seykota famously said that "everyone gets what they want from the markets". What is it that you *really* want?

Jérome Kerviel, the trader from Société Générale who lost $7.2 billion, was alleged to have said that all he wanted was to, "become an extraordinary trader". Did he achieve his goal? Do you think that this is really the outcome that he wanted? He is certainly extraordinary, and definitely received huge amounts of publicity and coverage across the globe.

It is always interesting when I ask trainees why it is that they want to be traders. Excitement and 'the buzz' is one of the most common answers they give. And yet, trading rarely turns out to be the adrenaline fuelled high-octane environment that they thought it would be – unless they are doing it badly! Trading can be very exciting, and highly adrenaline-fuelled, and not in the slightest bit profitable; so being clear on your motivations, and the impact of them on your trading, is key.

Trading also poses an interesting psychological challenge: commitment to a non-guaranteed outcome. When you place a trade you have no absolute idea of the actual outcome. You are at best playing probabilities (and at worst simply hoping!). Your trading results over time are a factor of the trades you place, and therefore it is impossible with any great degree of certainty to predict profitability and income levels; the outcomes of your trading are not totally under your control. When pursuing the trading path you will no doubt have some goals and outcomes that you would like to achieve – trading could well fulfil all of them and more, but there is no guarantee. Putting in significant amounts of effort over long periods of time can be difficult when there is no certain level of reward at the end. Indeed in trading you can work extremely hard and have periods of *no* financial reward. Can you imagine what would happen if that occurred in an ordinary job!

As a trader you need to have clear goals set out, have positive expectations and a high self-belief, be able to work hard over time, all the while knowing that you may – potentially – not achieve those goals at all, or not for some time.

Beyond Motivation – Drive

"If you turned up to trade and someone had boarded the door up in a cartoon fashion, what would you do? I'd smash through it. If you would choose to go home and come back/call later, stay at home."

– Matt Blom, futures trader

Motivation is powerful, as we know, but it can be variable and subject to our moods or events. Most top performers depend on something stronger: drive. This manifests itself in a real interest and love of trading – being fascinated and passionate about what you do. It underpins your ability to achieve, and helps to sustain strong focus over time; as well as giving you what K. Anders Ericsson, in his research on creating expertise, calls "the rage to master".

Drive, to me, is pure, and occurs when you are really engaged in your occupation and finally have a *natural* motivation – you are not having to motivate yourself.

Motivation will become drive given sufficient enthusiasm, time and hard work.

Exercise: Enhancing Motivation

Can you think of a time when you were really motivated to do something?

What were your thoughts? What did your inner dialogue and mental imagery consist of? What feelings did you have?

Holding strong mental pictures, combined with positive inner dialogue, can be a very powerful motivator! Take some time to identify your core trading motivations; write them down, and read through them regularly. As you do this, create a kind of mental image to represent each of the motives. Attach the same powerful associations to it that you experienced when you recalled your previous motivational event.

 Trader Top Tips

"Remember why you got into trading in the first place and what you hope to achieve from being here. Focus on your goals."

– Andrew Nuthall, oil trader

"Motivation is very important, especially early on. Remember why you wanted to be a trader, what it is you wanted to achieve. This will help to engender discipline and help you when times are tough."

– Stewart Hampton, trader

"I have written my own motivational statement at the start of my trading plan and have it pinned to the wall beside my computer. It's cobbled together from different readings and lessons I have gathered over my trading journey. It works for me."

– Brent Evans, trader

Practical Strategy: Reinforcing Your Motivation and Commitment

Make a list of your core trading motivations.

Read through the list regularly to reinforce your motivation and commitment to being a trader.

You can adapt this process by writing a powerful and compelling motivational statement/paragraph and reading through this.

STRATEGY 4

Develop a Compelling Vision of Trading Success

"Develop a vision, a compelling future that excites and inspires you, and focus on it daily."

– Anthony Robbins, motivational speaker

Success Starts With a Dream or Vision

Most successful people and high achievers started their journey with a dream, a compelling goal, or a purpose. Having a dream or purpose is important in maintaining long-term motivation and drive, and is often the deciding factor between people who give up, and those who carry on, when they face setbacks.

If your purpose or mission is big enough, no obstacle will get in your way.

Trading can become very consuming and a large part of your life. In the pursuit of achieving and sustaining trading success, it is easy to get tunnel vision and to narrow your attention onto trading and nothing else.

So one activity that I like to undertake with my own clients is the Design Your Life exercise. At times it can feel like trading is life; however, we must remember that trading is only a *part* of life. In order to provide balance, but also to provide a compelling future to work towards - to give a value and purpose to your hard work, and sustaining high performance in trading - it is very useful to take the time to consider and be clear about how you would like your life, in the round, to be. I was first introduced to this Design Your Life practice by Sportsmind director Jeffrey Hodges.

Plan Your Vision From the Future

"I like the dreams of the future better than the history of the past."

– Thomas Jefferson

Most people live life reacting to events - feeling as though they are acted upon, controlled by other people and external forces. It does not have to be that way. It is possible to feel in charge of your life, to feel as though you're the one deciding what you do, where you go, who you're with, and how you spend you time. The only way to achieve this is to decide now to design your life!

Your biggest challenge in completing this exercise will be in freeing yourself from the limitations and barriers that you impose on yourself based on what you have achieved to date and where you are right now. The past is not a determinant of the future. Yes, you are a result of genetics and conditioning over time; however, you are also a pre-consequence of a future you. In completing the 'Ideal Life' and 'Compelling Vision' exercises I urge you, in a sense, to go to the future, to rid yourself of your preconceptions and limitations, and write down how you really want things to be – to create your ideal life and not a "realistic" one, to create a compelling vision and not an ordinary one.

Design Your Life

When designing, it's important to consider the key aspects of your life. We might reduce these to five.

1. Health/fitness

2. Wealth/possessions

3. Career/achievements

4. Personal development/contribution

5. Relationships/family

Each of the five represents a different portion of your life. The first is your health and fitness – because if you don't have good health, you won't be able to achieve or enjoy anything else. The next two are wealth/possessions on the one hand, and career/achievements on the other. The final two are personal development/contribution, and relationships/family – because without a sense of contribution and growth, and connection with others, even great achievements feel hollow and meaningless.

So, let's start designing your life.

Practical Strategy: Design Your Life

If you could live where you wanted, do what you wanted, and be the person you most wanted to be, what would that look, sound and feel like?

Take the next 15 minutes to write down all your dreams and desires, as if they were really possible for you. Don't be concerned just yet about whether you can achieve something or not, or how you could go about it; we'll be considering these issues later on. For now, simply get all your dreams down.

To help, you might want to consider:

Where do you want to live?

What kind of home do you want?

What kind of car?

How much income do you want to earn in a year?

How much do you want to have in savings?

What places would you like to visit?

What have you always wanted to learn, or do, that you've never gotten around to yet?

What would you like to contribute to our society/the world?

Who do you want to know and be friends with?

How do you want your family to be?

How fit do you want to be?

What skills do you want to have?

What do you want to achieve in your career/trading?

What possessions do you yearn for?

And so on.

Write down your thoughts and ideas above, and then organise them and any other desires into the five groupings below and put them somewhere where you can consult them whenever you feel the need.

Health & Fitness

Wealth & Possessions

Career & Achievement

Personal Development & Contribution

Relationships & Family

STRATEGY 5

T.R.A.D.E. to Success – Goal Achievement Strategies

"If you don't know where you are going, you probably won't end up there."

– Yogi Berra

Where Are You Heading?

Setting clear, specific written goals can have an incredible effect on the levels of performance that you achieve. In *Sportsmind*, Jeffrey Hodges states that "only about 5% of people surveyed are goal setters and less than 1% have written down goals". Given how important definite goals are for focus, drive and motivation – the fuel for success – this means potentially that 95-99% of people are under-achieving. What about you?

"Write your goals down and break them into achievable targets. By doing this, it will help to motivate you no matter what stage you are at."

– Nigel Read, futures trader

Exercise: Goals Reflection

What are your trading goals?

Why are these goals important to you?

Are your goals clear and specific?

Are your goals written down?

Could a lack of clearly defined specific written goals be keeping you from maximising your performance potential? How much more could you be achieving?

If you are already setting clear, specific goals and writing them down – then fantastic! Keep up the good work. Keep reading, though, to see if you can improve on the process of setting goals, particularly if you have found that, whilst you are setting goals, you are having a tough time achieving them.

What Are Goals and Why Are They Important to Trading Performance?

"Why are you trading? As with any long-term pursuit, it's nice to have goals and rewards. What are you going to do with the money? Set small targets and reward yourself."

– Harold Cataquet, Cataquet and Associates Ltd

Goals are desired outcomes. They are what we would like to achieve.

You will have them, and have acted on them, whether you've done so consciously and deliberately or not. But they need to be carefully *set* – established on a precise and targeted footing – to be really effective.

Many traders ask me why they should set goals, what the benefits are? I have listed some of the really key ones below.

Key reasons to set goals

- Create motivation
- Give direction
- Enable feedback
- Enhance energy and provide inspiration
- Increase your effort and intensity
- Increase your levels of persistence when faced with challenges
- Help you to prioritise how you spend your resources of time/energy
- Enable you to develop strategies and action plans to move forwards
- Generate creative tension! (The gap between internal desire and reality – this further enables the drive to make the changes to get from where you are to where you want to be)

Why Do People Not Set Goals?

If goals have so many positive benefits, it is interesting to reflect on why so few people set them. Below are five typical reasons why people choose not to set goals.

5 reasons people don't set goals

- *Not bothered.* Some people just simply do not want to put the time and effort into setting goals.

- *Unaware of the benefits.* Many traders have not been introduced to the power of goal achievement processes, as training for traders is primarily centred around the development of job specific skills, and performance skills are typically left out.

- *Don't know how.* Little training is given to traders on how to set goals effectively.

- *Fear of failure.* For most people, setting goals has an anxiety attached to it. What if I don't achieve the goal? For many, this doubt is fatal. Instead they assume that if they don't set a goal and then get something good, it will be a nice surprise; and if things don't work out, then it won't be as disappointing.

- *Fear of success.* For a few traders, the fear of being successful and what that may bring can be enough to lead them to not set goals.

Goal Setting vs. Goal Achievement

Something I really want to stress is that this chapter is actually really about goal achievement, not simply goal-setting. Anyone can set a goal. Achieving the goal is the real challenge, and therefore the thing to focus on when establishing them. It is a two-part process and requires determination.

In his book *Motivated Mind* Dr Raj Persaud states that research shows that over 50% of New Year's resolutions are broken before the end of January. And by February 28, only 25% of people have maintained their resolutions – but, interestingly, it is in fact quite likely that the majority of these people will then be able to sustain their progress, as they have already gone through 60-odd days of 'conditioning'. So the gap between the diligent and the defeated is narrow but decisive.

Being a goal setter, or being a goal achiever. Which sounds best? Which would you rather be?

Think of goals that you have set for yourself, but have not achieved or followed through on. Why was that? Now think of goals that you have achieved and followed through on. Why was *that*?

Achieving goals is a process – a personal management process. Often we do not achieve our goals because the goals are not set effectively. This can be remedied.

TRADE to Success

The fundamentals of the goal achievement process are:

- Knowing specifically what you want to achieve, and what achieving it will be like.

- Knowing why you want to achieve your goal, and why you can achieve it.

- Creating an action plan for achieving your goal.

- Taking action, and noticing the feedback as you move towards achieving it.

- It is really important that, once you have decided on your goals, you write them down. This act makes them important. You are then committing to them. Additionally, some people find that, by sharing their goal with someone else, their adherence to the required achievement process is enhanced.

- The TRADE model can be useful in helping you to identify your goals and plan their accomplishment.

Practical Strategy: TRADE to Success

Target – what specifically do you want to achieve? When, where, with whom? How will you know when you have achieved this? Write your goal in the positive: what you want and not what you are trying to avoid.

(contd.)

R easons – why is achieving this goal important to you? *(Think back to STRATEGY 4, and designing your life. Think also in terms, though, of personal excellence and improvement.)*

A ction – what action will you take/what needs to happen? Are there any possible obstacles?

D o – take action!

E valuate – when and how will you keep track of your progress? *(See STRATEGY 26)*

Key Time Horizons for Goal-Setting

When you look to set goals it can be useful to consider three time horizons under which to organise them. Based on the Sportsmind model I have used with athletes very successfully, I employ the same framework with traders, looking at goals over 2-5 years, 12 months, and the more immediate future.

Always start with the furthest away goals first and then work back. Writing your 2-5 year goals will probably be your biggest challenge. It is likely that you will set those goals based on what you feel is possible, as evidenced by what has historically happened, rather than allowing yourself the freedom and creativity of setting some exciting and compelling goals. We are frequently reminded of how we are who we are because of what has happened to us and how the past has shaped the present. However, here is my challenge to you: you also have lots of room to be shaped and developed, and the future is not yet set; so establish your longer-term goals from an idealistic perspective, and allow yourself the challenge of achieving them. Let them be inspirational

> **"You have lots of room to be shaped and developed, and the future is not yet set. Set yourself realistic short-term, but idealistic long-term, challenges. "**

and motivational. 2-5 years is a long time and so much can happen over such a time frame; cast your mind back 2-5 years and look at all that has happened in that time since. Break out of the limitations of the past and set the goals you *want*, not the goals you feel you *can* accomplish. It is in the shorter term that the goals need to become more realistic.

There are also three types of goals that you want to be aware of – outcome goals, performance goals and process goals. Outcome goals are the end result, e.g. your P&L, number of ticks, etc. Performance goals are objective measures and would include, for example, your number of winning trades/losing trades, average winner/loser, Sharpe ratio, etc. Process goals are specific actions, behaviours, feelings and processes required to achieve the desired outcome. In essence, if outcome goals are the jigsaw picture, then process goals are the pieces.

All three types of goals are important to success because, without a clearly defined and desired outcome, motivation lags, and there is a loss of direction. However, without the process goals – the actions – there is less chance of achieving the outcome! What is important is knowing when to focus on the outcome, and when to focus on the process.

Your process goals should all be under your direct control, and will include what you want to be doing and being. *Doing* will include areas such as your preparation, how you are picking and entering trades, how you manage trades, how you are exiting trades, how you are evaluating. *Being* goals might include feelings and thoughts.

"The only way to trade effectively is to make oneself accountable by creating structure; but with accountability comes responsibility."

– Mark Douglas, *The Disciplined Trader*

Process goals tend to be more memorable and inspiring when they are written in the present tense and positively phrased – before being mentally rehearsed and visualised.

Example Process Goals

- I am coming to the office feeling energised, positive and expecting to make money.

- I am doing my preparation – updating my market knowledge and performing my routines.

- I am entering trades according to my trading strategy.

- I am feeling calm, confident and composed during my trades.

"I have found that making a poster with images that reflect my goals really helps me to stay focussed on my vision from day to day. Deciding on your goals and then finding the pictures to represent them makes the whole process more creative."

– S.P., trader

Practical Strategy: Goal Achievement Strategy

Having written down your most important outcome goals, organise them for 1-3 months, 12 months and 2-5 years. Use the TRADE model as a framework for your process. Then mark them up – perhaps using different colours – as to whether they are outcome, performance or process goals. Make an action plan, that you can daily or weekly refer to, which says what you will do today, tomorrow, next week, next month to achieve them.

It may also help to write a paragraph on why you want to achieve these goals. What are your reasons for wanting them? How would you feel if you didn't achieve them? How are you going to feel when you do achieve them?

STRATEGY 6

Know Who You Need to Become

"The successful trader that you want to become is a future
'projection' of yourself, for you to grow into."

– Mark Douglas, *Trading in the Zone*

One of the key questions I ask my coaching clients when going through the goal-setting process, once we have the goals clearly defined, is: "*Who* do you need to become to achieve that goal?"

Achieving a goal is a moment in time in the future, and the achievement of that goal will depend on the trader having the skill, knowledge, attitudes and behaviours to be able to meet the expectations set. Naturally, the trader will then be different in some way to how he is now; if he already had everything in place then he would presently be achieving his goal, and we would not be meeting or going through this process.

So, to achieve a goal in the future there will be a requirement at some level to make a change or changes. The process becomes transformational – the trader will essentially be going through a process of change until they become able to achieve their goal.

"For me the most important concept that must be understood is what do I have to *become* to be a successful trader? All other advice falls down in the long run, if this isn't implemented, understood and lived by."

— Matt Blom, trader

Consider the future you as a sculpture, and the present and developing you as the sculptor. A sculptor holds in their mind a vision of their finished piece of work, and is constantly refining and working with their material to bring it ever closer to that vision. Having a future vision of yourself as a successful trader enables you to identify what you need to personally work on and develop in order to get closer, bit by bit, to that goal.

Robert Dilts has helpfully broken this personal process down into six levels or components, and it may be useful to employ these as a basis for your plan.

The Future Trader You

1. Mission
What is your purpose in becoming a trader?

2. Identity
Who will you be as the ideal trader? Describe yourself as a trader.

3. Beliefs and Values
What beliefs about trading will you have? Markets? Self? Success? Money? Trading? Why is trading important to you?

4. Capabilities and Skills
What skills and capabilities will you have acquired?

5. Behaviours
How will you be behaving/what will you be doing?

6. Environment
What will your environment be like?

So, given the above, what specific actions do you need to take to move towards the future you? Incorporate them into your goals.

STRATEGY 7

Find Your Magic – Developing Your Trading Strategy

"Without a trading system you are floating aimlessly in a sea of opportunity with no land in sight."

– Mark Douglas, *The Disciplined Trader*

Why Strategy Matters

There are only really two technical keys to achieving success in trading – firstly, developing a trading strategy with an edge in the market, and secondly, developing the ability to consistently execute that strategy.

Developing a trading strategy or approach that has an edge in the market is the first and most fundamental goal in trading. Without this you are, as Mark Douglas puts it, "floating aimlessly" in a generally haphazard and random adventure. Consistency will be hard to come by, except insofar as you may find yourself consistently losing money.

The 2 keys to successful trading

Trading strategy with an edge + the ability to consistently execute that strategy

Exercise: Where Are You and What Are Your Needs?

Take a moment to reflect on your trading – where you are in terms of strategy, and consistency of execution.

Which quadrant are you in?

	Consistent Execution	Inconsistent Execution
Strategy Trade	1	2
Non-Strategy Trade	3	4

Quadrant 1 – high quality trading. You have a defined trading strategy and are consistently executing it. Your goal is to keep focussed on trading your strategy – be mindful of times when you have strings of losses or winners and also of the possible need to adapt and refine your strategy over time. Part 3 of this book will have chapters with significant importance for you.

Quadrant 2 – undisciplined trading. The key goal here is to develop your ability to execute your strategy consistently and so it is likely that there may be a psychological aspect to explore and to develop. Part 2 of this book will have significant value for you.

Quadrant 3 – consistent random trading (also know as 'gambling'!). Stop! Your absolute key focus has to be on developing a trading strategy with an edge in the market and a positive expectancy. This chapter is critical for you.

Quadrant 4 – inconsistent random trading (again, gambling). This haphazard approach is not going to bring consistent profitability over time. This chapter is critical for you.

Without a profitable trading strategy it does not mean that you cannot make money. But with a more random approach, although you will undoubtedly get some winning trades, and maybe even some big ones, you are also likely to take some big losses, and not achieve a consistent return over time.

Anyone can achieve short-term wins in trading through luck and randomness alone. As a good fellow trainer friend of mine, Jonno Sharpe, says, "Even a blind squirrel finds nuts sometimes!" Our goal as high performance traders is to achieve consistency of performance over time and to control as many of the controllables as we can.

Having a strategy defines when there are or are not trading opportunities. It sets the parameters for you to trade by, to be accountable to, and to measure your progress and performance.

Developing a Trading Strategy

The ability to develop a trading strategy is a skill that could fill a book on its own. There are, however, some fundamental points to consider, and we will touch on these here to get you started on the right path.

It is common for newer traders to adopt a standardised approach to their trading, utilising a strategy or style that someone else has taught them. This is a starting point, and is rather like learning to drive; everyone learns the core skills in a basic car. You need to get behind the wheel and get going.

> **“ Developing a trading strategy is a key skill to learn: nothing stays still, and you will have to call upon it when markets change. ”**

Over time, though, drivers will individualise their driving style and the cars they drive. Over time, traders should likewise be looking to refine and individualise their trading style, and perhaps, where appropriate, the markets they trade. The process of going from a standardised approach to an individualised one is part of the pathway to trading success. Indeed I have seen myself that sometimes it is clinging on to the standardised approaches, and not recognising the importance of beginning to individualise, that ultimately holds some traders back.

It is very rare that I meet a successful and experienced trader who is still trading the same strategy that they learned with. In fact, even within a few months most professional traders are beginning to individualise their styles and approaches, even when they may all have been on the same graduate course, and been taught the same strategy, by the same people, in the same way.

Learning how to develop a trading strategy is important not least because nothing stays still. The markets are dynamic and ever changing – over time you will need to be able to adapt your style and strategy in response to this. I have unfortunately seen too many traders lose large sums of money – and, for some, their careers – due to an inability to adapt and respond to changes in market conditions. Having the ability to develop a trading strategy is therefore, from every point of view, a key factor in creating longevity in the markets.

> "In warfare there are no constant conditions. He who can modify his tactics in relation to his opponent will succeed and win."
>
> **– Sun-Tzu, *The Art of War***

When you are looking to develop or adapt a trading strategy there are many aspects to consider and work through. (See 'Developing Your Trading Strategy'.) Broadly, the process will be:

- Starting with an idea or theme – what is the trading concept?

- Selecting your market(s)

- Deciding upon the time frame you will trade over

- Defining your entry indicators and exit criteria

- Evaluating the system – back and forward testing

- Refining the system based on the feedback you receive

Developing Your Trading Strategy

Create an outline of your trading strategy.

You may find it helpful to consider the following points:

- What is your core trading idea or theme?

- Are there any sub-themes/ideas?

- What market will you/would you like to trade? And why?

- What time frame will you trade over?

- What will your style of trading be?

- How will you be using technical/fundamental analysis?

- Define the key elements of your strategy in relation to the five stage trade process - monitor/spot/enter/manage/exit/post-trade

- What will your risk and money management strategy be?

- How will you structure your trading session?

- What edge(s) do you have in the market (knowledge, skills, execution, psychological)?

- What strengths do you have as a trader? How will you utilise them?

- What weaknesses do you have as a trader? How will you overcome them?

- What contingency plans do you have – losing day; series of losing trades/days?

- How will you manage the mental and emotional aspects of trading?

- How will you evaluate your performance and progress?

- What are the costs of trading – fixed and variable? Commissions? Trading system? Charting packages? New feeds? Subscriptions? Rentals/facilities?

N.B. It is important to consider that this trading strategy should also be a reflection of you and your trading philosophy, goals and motivations, which we established earlier.

Finding Your Magic!

There is no magic formula – well, there is, but the magic is different for everyone.

I remember once speaking at a trading symposium. Before my slot there were some live trading demonstrations from five well-regarded and successful traders and coaches, with the audience being able to ask questions as they traded. Do you know what the most asked question was? All variations of "What is the magic indicator/system that makes you money most often?" Interestingly, the traders all gave different answers, and some were polar opposites!

Whilst the audience were so hooked on finding the holy grail, they missed the entire point, and perhaps the most significant lesson of the whole symposium – that there is no magic system, but there is a system, a style and an approach that will work best for you. Finding this is, if anything, the trader's holy grail – although, of course, the markets are dynamic, so such things never stay still for long.

Instead, you must develop the ability to consistently devise new strategies; to, in a sense, regularly bottle your magic formula in different vessels for different times, trends and markets.

"Not whether you can be a good trader, but whether you can find the trading that is good for you."

– Brett Steenbarger, Enhancing Trader Performance

Are all people suited to and therefore likely to excel in the same jobs or careers? Are all people suited to and therefore likely to excel in the same sports? Are all people suited to and therefore likely to excel at playing the same instrument? The answer of course is no.

So are all people suited to and therefore likely to excel at the same style of trading? Of course, again, the answer is an emphatic no. There are many different markets to trade and many different ways in which to trade them. One of the key developmental goals of any trader is to find the style of trading and market that best matches them, their personality, goals and motivations and trading philosophy.

A question I am often asked is "How do I know if I am trading the best market and style for me?" The same question could be asked regarding employment choices, an academic subject being studied, or a particular sport being played. We might use some key indicators to help us monitor this, including:

- Motivation – do you want to do what you are doing?
- Strengths – do you feel that what you are doing is playing to your strengths?
- Interests – are you interested in what you are doing?
- Performance and Results – are your performance and results indicative of high performance or the potential for it?

Much of this information is going to be collated through your trading records and logs, etc.

Where traders are working in teams or are part of an organisation, there is the possibility of getting external feedback from trader managers, trainers and coaches. This can be extremely valuable, not least because past experience and historical studies can be used.

A further area that I have explored in my own work is the use of psychometric testing (measuring factors such as decision-making speed, intuitive ability, analytical ability, information processing, risk propensity, concentration and focus, emotional flexibility) to help to identify a trader's particular performance style. We then use this alongside any observational and recorded data to help move traders in the right direction.

This approach has proven to be very effective. On several occasions, traders who were struggling to achieve consistent profitability and success in one market and with one style, have been moved to a different market and/or style. And, within relatively short periods of time, they have showed significant improvements in their trading results. Several have gone on to become successful traders, whereas at one time they may have been one trade away from a different role or career!

Finding your niche is going to be the result of a combination of ongoing assessment, getting feedback from others, and time/experience. To help you start thinking about where you are now, and where your magic may be, complete the following exercises.

Exercise: Finding Your Magic

Take some time to reflect on your trading and answer the following questions:

Strengths

What do you naturally enjoy?

What do you naturally do well?

What do significant others perceive in you?

Interests

What are you naturally interested in?

Motivation

What are you most passionate about?

Performance

What do you feel you can be best at?

Results

Where do you feel you could be most profitable?

What did you notice?

Are you currently acting in line with your findings? Where? Where not?

How could you utilise your strengths, interests, skills and talents more effectively?

Treat Your Trading as a Business

"Do not underestimate the costs of trading – you have overheads, fixed costs, variable costs, just like any business."

– Nick Shannon, occupational psychologist

Trading is too often treated casually, or as a hobby. The result of trading as a mere pastime can often turn out to be very costly and frustrating.

To increase your chances of success and to be super-effective as a trader, trading should be treated as a business, and then run accordingly. This applies to full-time professionals as well as the long-term investor who does not trade with frequency.

Real Life Example

I was delivering a seminar at a conference for retail traders, when I was approached by one of the delegates at the interval. He started to tell me about his own journey in trading. He had lost over £10,000 in the first few months, he said, so he had soon stopped and taken some time out of the markets. His biggest realisation was that he didn't actually know much about trading after all – what it really involved, what the costs genuinely were, and, importantly, what the risks were.

I asked him what he did for a living. He replied that he ran two very successful businesses. I asked him how he had created such success. He explained that he had found a potential niche to exploit, done lots of research, undergone some extra training and education, and then devised his business plan, before seeking funding and support for his venture. I asked him if he felt he had been thorough in his preparation before actually launching his businesses. "Yes," he replied, "you have to be. The risk of not being thorough is just too great." I then asked him to reflect on what his approach to his trading had been like, in comparison with his approach to his business start-ups.

Obviously they had been *very* different!

I have seen many people getting sucked into trading without having a really good understanding of what they are getting into, and what the potential risks and associated costs are. I have, as a result of this, met many people who have lost a lot of money in the markets – when most of these losses could have been reduced or even avoided.

For all traders I really feel that it is important that you view your trading as a business. We are after all dealing with profit and loss; we are investing time and energy, and in some cases our trading capital, into getting a financial return. There are costs of business with software licenses, charting package fees, commissions (or the spread), desk fees, etc, and there are revenues – profits and in some cases rebates.

So the mindset of operating your trading activities as a business can be very productive.

STRATEGY 8

Identify Your Critical Performance Factors

"Performance is the culmination of doing all the things that are right."

– Larry Pasavento

Know What Matters

Imagine waking up one day and thinking to yourself, "I am going to run a marathon". You set off on a seemingly thorough training programme – going to the gym, lifting weights, doing some cycling and a few short runs.

After 16 weeks of such training you arrive at the starting line, looking and feeling great. But with less than half the race gone, you struggle to keep going. You eventually stop and have to walk the rest of the way. Why? Although you had a goal to run the marathon and you committed time and energy towards achieving that goal, you did not focus that time and energy into activities that were critical to its *particular kind of performance*, in this case endurance running.

As a trader it is very important to identify what the *critical* performance factors are for you. This will enable you to direct your time and focus appropriately in order to maximise your trading performance and profitability. Time and energy spent on non-critical factors simply detracts from performance.

Tune In

We are always focussed – the question is on *what*. Your ability to focus on what's important – the right thing at the right time – and to be able to block out everything else, is one of the primary keys to trading success. In their book *The Trading Athlete*, Shane Murphy and Doug Hirschhorn refer to this as "tuning in". It can be vital.

What factors do you need to focus on to trade to your very best? What are you focussed on when you are monitoring the markets? What do you focus on when you spot an opportunity? What are you focussed on when you enter and then manage the trade? What do you focus on after the trade? How will you refocus should you lose concentration at any given time?

"When a trader is aware of exactly what they should be focussed on, and has the ability to focus on it in an almost altered state such as that of a samurai, he has mastered mental toughness."

– S.P., trader

In the trading execution process we have six core components:

1. Monitor – watching the markets

2. Spot – spotting a trading opportunity

3. Enter – enter the market, place the trade

4. Manage – management of the position

5. Exit – close the position out

6. Post – evaluating the trade

In flawless execution, the trader focusses on the process of each of the six steps and aims to do each one as well as they possibly can. This will involve knowing what thoughts, feelings and behaviours/actions are desired at each stage. They evaluate their trading performance against the quality of their execution of the trade, alongside its profitability.

"Be focussed on the process to eliminate negative emotions."

– Matt Blom

Exercise: Performance Comparative Analysis

Bring to mind a time when you were trading but not very well, and another time when you were trading really well – a peak time.

Think seriously about the time when you were not trading well. What do you remember? What were you doing? What were you saying to yourself? What feelings did you have? As you remember it, really take time to notice your attitudes and behaviours. As you are going through this process, make a note of all the key factors that contributed to your performance. Record your findings below.

Now repeat this process for the time when you were trading really well. What do you remember? What was going through your mind? What were you doing? What feelings were you experiencing? Write down your findings again.

Now sit and reflect upon the experience, and undertake a comparative analysis by looking at the two different experiences and noting what differences there are.

So what factors appear to be critical to you performing well?

And what can you do to ensure that they are a regular part of your trading?

Things that might come to mind may include:

- Level of knowledge and understanding of trading and the markets
- Having a trading strategy that has an edge/positive expectancy and that you believe in
- Risk and money management
- Discipline in your trading execution – sticking to your strategy
- Being prepared and ready to trade
- Having had enough sleep
- Feeling confident and that you can make money

Also, consider over a longer time period which factors will have a significant impact on the achievement of your short, medium and long-term trading goals.

Things that may come to mind here could be:

- Setting and evaluating goals on a regular basis
- Having a trading plan
- Continual improvement and training
- Individualising your trading plan to suit your own strengths, interests, trading style and personality
- Putting in sufficient time and effort

- Maintaining discipline over time
- Sustaining motivation and energy levels

Real Life Example: Trader Critical Factors

(by S.P., trader)

Peak Trading Factors

trading my strategy and managing risk

health is good

preparing for the day with 'what if?' scenarios and targets

time to self in the morning before trading

thought process is 'let it happen' – flow of energy

process-focussed – letting the trades come to me

Poor Trading Factors

not well – smoking and drinking more

at desk constantly

not eating well or drinking enough water

waking up late

trade more than one market

get stuck in market direction and lose my flexibility

get frantic and tense with self and others

scared of missing out on opportunities

Focus On What Makes a Difference

In my work with traders and elite performers in other areas I have seen at first hand the importance of being able to focus time and energy (both of which are finite!) on the *critical* factors.

Sometimes we can get distracted from doing what we know we should be doing, or sometimes we may not be fully conscious of what those factors may be, perhaps due to lack of experience, and so on. However, as you progress through your trading journey, you will become more and more aware of what your critical factors are. A really important and easy way to capture these is through the regular use and evaluation of trade logs, journals and metrics.

Practical Strategy: Critical Performance Factors

Make a list of your critical trading performance factors and formulate rules for your trading process based on them. Use this as a checklist during your trading preparation and execution. Direct your time and energy during the trading session to focussing on what is important to producing your best performances.

When you get to the end of a trading session/day ask yourself, "Did I focus on the critical factors today?" Look at where you did and where you didn't. Commit to greater focus the next day if required.

Trader Performance Process	
Focus Question	**Rules**
Pre/Watch	
What is the nature of the market? – Time of day – Visible major players – Releases/speakers	
Spot	
What am I looking for that is an opportunity to trade? – Indicators and weighting	
Enter	
What reasons do I have for entering this trade, or for not entering? – Conviction – Risk/reward – Trade history	

(contd.)	
Focus Question	**Rules**
Manage	
What indicators am I looking at to monitor my trade? What Qs will I ask myself? How will I stay objective? When would I change my exit?	
Exit	
How will I know when to get out?	
Post	
How will I evaluate my trade?	

STRATEGY 9

Be P.R.E.Pared!

"The profitability of any fishing trip was often decided at the time of leaving the wharf, without even putting one hook in the water."

– Chris Collecut, trader (ex-offshore fisherman)

Are You Ready?

Imagine you are sitting on a plane waiting to take off and fly to some beautiful holiday destination. As you are sitting there you see what appears to be the pilot rush on board. You overhear him explaining to one of the air stewards that he feels awful, having overslept due to not going to bed till a few hours ago. In order to keep to the flight schedule he will, he yawns, be skipping the pre-flight checks, and just get going.

How do you feel?

Does the pilot's apparent lack of preparation worry you? If so, why?

Exercise: Current Trading Preparation Reflection

What do you do to prepare before you trade?

Take a moment to describe your preparation routine.

Are you consistent with this? If not, when do you do your preparation, and when don't you?

> "Winning is the science of being prepared."
>
> – George Allen

Top sports people and teams, businesses, the military, and top traders wanting to perform well with consistency have long recognised the importance of meticulous preparation. This high level of preparation pre-performance enables them to execute to the highest level possible.

"Most wizard traders engage in extensive research and preparation before trades."

– The New Market Wizards, Jack Schwager

Using a sports analogy, a team preparing for a big game will do everything possible to prepare themselves – technical training, tactics, fitness, nutrition, psychology, assessing strengths and weaknesses, looking at past performance, practising. *And*, importantly, they will also be spending time getting to know as much as is possible about their opponents – tactics, strengths and weaknesses, patterns, fitness, and so on. To trade to your full potential each time you will want to know as much as you can about yourself, and your 'opponent' – the markets.

What do average traders and average sports people have in common? They both generally spend less time and energy on preparing to perform than do good-to-exceptional traders and athletes. You only need to see the casual gym goer perform their quick leg shake and arm jiggle to know that all they really want to do is get on some machine and start 'exercising', just as in the same way the average trader only wants to get in front of the screen and get involved in the market.

Top performers in sports, the performing arts, trading and the military all have some kind of pre-performance routine to get them ready. Traders should be no different. Becoming a high-performance trader will involve you adopting performance habits that most other traders may get bored with or feel uncomfortable doing. Preparation is a key component of the performance cycle; it keeps you in a feedback loop that is essential to continual improvement and, ultimately, goal achievement.

The Benefits of Being Prepared

"Before everything else, getting ready is the secret of success."

– Henry Ford

Let's look firstly at the benefits of having such a routine, and then secondly at the components of what may be included within that routine.

What are the benefits of preparation?

"It is important to feel prepared – like an athlete prepping for a 100m final."

– Nick McDonald, Trade With Precision

Consistency

Repeating the same process each time before you trade is consistency of behaviour, and performance is ultimately an aggregate of behaviour. Getting into the habit of preparing each time you trade gives you the opportunity to establish consistency.

Confidence

Knowing that you have prepared can give you a real confidence boost – and knowing that you have not prepared or have under prepared can certainly give you an uneasy feeling! You only need a small part of you to know that you are under-prepared to create inner doubt and potential conflict, which can affect your trading execution. Each trader's preparation will be dependent on the markets they are trading, their style of trading, etc. However, for each there will be some optimum amount of preparation that is required.

❝ Preparation builds consistency, boosts confidence, and assures composure. It is self-control. ❞

Control

Preparation is a part of the trading day over which *you* have full control. What you prepare and how well you do it is entirely down to you!

Composure

If you have prepared fully and considered some 'what if?' scenarios, then one big edge is that your level of preparedness will enable you to act quickly and calmly should those events occur.

I witnessed this first hand at a trading institution in 2007, when the Fed made a surprise announcement and only two traders out of the 30 on the trading floor were able to react quickly and decisively enough to get in early on the market move. Both of those traders made large sums of money that day due to the fact that they had been prepared for such an event, and had considered what they would do in such a situation. Of the other traders in the room, most made little money and were left just watching the markets move.

Concentration

Your preparation routine can become a trigger to activate a focussed trading mindset. In sports, most players have a pre-performance routine – this is readily seen in golf, for example – and this routine enables them to switch their focus to the key performance factors and to get ready to engage in execution.

Transition

Going through your preparation routine also enables you to mentally shift from one mindset and state to another; e.g. from waking up to trading, or working to trading. It is important to make sure that when you are trading you are in trader mode.

Reduced risk

Knowing what is coming out in the markets in terms of economic data, speakers, earnings releases, auctions, etc is very important because any of these can have an impact on the market, and often the result is increased volatility around these areas. Knowing what is coming out and when, and considering the effects on the market, can help you to adjust your strategy or approach accordingly, and can help to mitigate any potential risks.

Practical Strategy – P.R.E.P.

Plan and prepare

Read through your trading strategy – big picture.

How will you apply it in this particular trading period?

Research economic data, speakers, figures, possible market conditions, your overall trading strategy/approach/processes and formulate a strategy for the day (am/pm); any levels you may be trading off, etc.

Rehearse

Mentally rehearse implementing your strategy, including dealing with the below 'what ifs'.

Eventualities

Consider 'what if?' scenarios that could arise from your strategy, and what you will do if those situations *do* arise. This is a very important step. You are preparing for adversity, for dealing with difficult market conditions.

Positive state

Check you are in a positive state before you trade – use a simple 0-10 scale (0 = very poor state, 10 = ideal trading state).

Example Routine Components to Calibrate

Nutrition – breakfast, energy snacks, light lunch, water (STRATEGY 14)

Exercise – cardio exercise, which stimulates the mind; walk or exercise before trading period commences (STRATEGY 14)

Positive self-talk/affirmations (STRATEGIES 23 and 34)

Asking powerful questions such as "What is going well for me?" "What am I grateful for today?"

Breathing exercises

Preparation

STRATEGY 10

Create a High-Performance Environment

"Surround yourself with the right people in a healthy
environment."

– Jerry Lynch, *The Way of the Champion*

Creating a Powerful Trading Team

In Jack Canfield's book *The Success Principles* he argues that "[y]ou are the average of the five people you spend the most time with." Interesting. Let's assume it to be true. What does this mean for you?

Exercise: Trading Team Assessment

Who are the five people you spend the most time with?

1.   2.   3.

4.   5.

What is the likely impact of this on you? What about in the context of trading?

What if you were the average of the five traders/trading-related people that you spent the most time with?

What is the implication of this for you as a trader?

Are you spending time with people who have a positive influence on you and your trading? Or is their influence less useful?

What qualities would you actively seek in people if you had to choose them as your Top 5?

What about qualities in people that you would not choose?

Groups of people, just like teams, have cultures – a way of being and doing – which are a powerful influence on performance. I have witnessed the power of culture on performance in my work with sports teams, sales teams, businesses and with groups, teams and organisations of traders. Culture, a set of beliefs and values which is held and purveyed throughout an organisation, drives the behaviours and therefore the performances of those it encompasses.

How would you describe the culture where you work and trade?

What are the beliefs and values that are held and how do they influence behaviour and performance?

Is it positive and performance-enhancing?

Building a positive performance-focussed culture is something that I am always aiming to do when I work with traders. This means identifying a set of beliefs and values, and importantly an overriding mission or purpose to drive everything. As a trader yourself it can have a huge impact on your level of achievement and success if you have a culture around you that supports and facilitates this.

Undoubtedly there have been traders who have been less talented than others, who have nevertheless become very successful as a result of the cultures in which they have worked. And on the flipside there will have been many competent traders who have underperformed because of the culture that surrounded them.

We do not all have the power to create a culture, as this is generally done top-down and over time. However, each of us are a part of that culture, and maybe within our smaller teams and desks we can have more impact, and drive a positive high-performance culture. For traders trading their own accounts, and operating more independently, you have the opportunity to actually build your team around you, and to do that based upon the culture that you want to operate in.

British Cycling over recent years has developed into *the* major force on the track, totally dominating at both world and Olympic competitions. Their rise to success has not been random, and it has not been left to luck. It has been planned and developed, but importantly it has then been *driven* by a culture of excellence and desire for peak performance – headed by Dave Brailsford, but with a team of coaches and support staff and athletes who all live by the same set of beliefs and values, and who are driven by the same compelling mission. Below are some key points to take away from the British Cycling culture that I feel any trader, trading team or organisations would do well to include in their own approach:

- Take nothing for granted, focus solely on being the best that you can be and spend little time wondering what the opposition is doing – don't take the winning periods or big winning trades for granted, spend little time worrying about other traders you know and how much money they are making.

- Phenomenal attention to detail – I know of many very successful traders who show this trait. Making sure that they have good front-end trading systems, access to the information that they need, and are continuing to work on developing all of the required skills and knowledge required.

- It's also about a fascination with the process of achieving excellence rather than with the reward itself. *What does it take to achieve excellence as a trader?* What do you need to do to achieve that level – what do you need to keep doing, what do you need to stop doing, and what do you need to start doing? The theme here, as I have stressed before, is a focus on excellence in process and not on outcome! That will be taken care of by default, if the first is attended to.

- The one question at the root of everything in the GB Cycling team is: "Can we win a gold medal?" or "Will this activity or action help us gain a gold?" If the answer to that is no, they simply don't do it. For traders, that question might well be "Will it make me a better trader?" And if it will, then do it; if not, then don't.

In building your network, trading community or group it might pay to give some thought to who you spend time with and how much time you spend with them. In building your team, aim for a culture that is based on the things that you most wish to develop and see in yourself as a trader. Focus on a positive and high-performance culture, one that will best facilitate the achievement of your trading goals.

Creating Your Physical Trading Environment

"Things such as where you work, where you sit and who you sit by are really important decisions for a trader and can have a big impact on their performance."

– David Helps, LIFFE

I remember working with a Vendée Globe participant (a single-handed round-the-world sailor). I went to the Isle of Wight to work with him for the day, and we took a trip to the docks to see the yacht that he would be sailing. I recall being very impressed by the external look of the boat – big, fast, sleek, hi-tech – and then being even more impressed by the interior. It was incredibly small and cramped; essentially just a small cockpit to sail from and live in for all those months at sea. Yet he had not spared any detail in designing and adjusting it to meet his needs.

It was remarkable. The seat was specially functional (he had to sleep in it as well as work from it), the layout was efficient and effective, and even the colour (which was mixed by colour specialists in the US) was developed to sustain a positive psychological state. It served as a useful reminder about the power of environment on performance. He had spent time and money to ensure that the internal environment was as conducive to high performance as possible – he made certain that what might seem perfunctory was actually perfectly adapted for success. Traders ought to bear this lesson in mind.

- What is your trading environment like?

- Is it conducive to you achieving your best trading results?

- What is the layout of your desk?

- What about the room where you trade?

- Your screensavers on the PC?

- Photographs/pictures/paintings near you?

- Functionality – screen placement, chair, keyboard and mouse positioning (ergonomics)?

When I first came into trading it was to work with a very large trading organisation in London. My first visit was to their head office in London, a fantastic building right in the heart of the City. The reception area was very smart, fitted out with plasma screens and designer furniture; the trading floor was full of high tech kit, with ergonomically designed chairs, motivational pictures on the wall, and glass panels; and a games room, a concierge service and a café rounded things off. The environment was exemplary.

For those traders working from a shared office, there will be some restrictions as to what you can do to the trading environment. However, most should be able to have a good say in the set out of their trading desk. For those trading from home, you will have more control over the design and layout of your trading environment. One thing that I would certainly recommend where appropriate and possible is having a separate trading desk/area – this is important in helping the mind to focus on the required task at hand, with minimal external distraction.

Take some time to create the best possible trading environment for yourself – it's easy to do and makes a big difference.

Practical Strategy: Creating a High-Performance Environment

- Seating – invest in a good quality chair with back/lumbar support.

- Lighting – natural lighting is desirable versus artificial and especially fluorescent lighting.

- Heat – a comfortable environment is important. If you are too hot or too cold then not only will this distract you but you are also placing additional stress on your body, and therefore on the mind. If you are using air conditioning then remember to drink more water to compensate for the extra dehydration effect.

- Noise – a quiet area free of distraction.

- Images – motivational or inspiring pictures on the wall (if necessary, browse the web for inspiration and either print your own, or get one of numerous website stores to professionally print and frame them).

Part Two

Decision–Making, Discipline and Flawless Execution

STRATEGY 11

Discipline and Your Ideal Trading State

"Be wary of the Dark Side!"

– Sonny Schneider

The Big 'D' – Discipline

Anyone who has traded or has read about trading will be familiar with the word discipline. In *New Market Wizards*, Jack Schwager found that, "[d]iscipline was probably the most frequent word used by the exceptional traders that I interviewed. Often it was mentioned in an almost apologetic tone: 'I know you've heard this a million times before, but believe me, it's really important'."

But what is it?

What is trading discipline?

How would you define it?

Most people, when I ask them that question, suggest that it is the ability to be able to consistently execute your trading strategy and to follow your trading rules, and this may also be inclusive of completing trading disciplines such as preparation and evaluation.

Let us consider the two keys to successful trading from earlier:

1. Having a strategy with an edge and a positive expectancy.

2. Being able to consistently execute the strategy.

It is the second of these that we are concerned with, although we must remember that being disciplined enough to put in the work to develop a trading strategy with an edge is obviously required.

Richard Dennis who created the Turtle Trading project once made the following observation:

> I always say that you could publish my trading rules in the newspaper and no one would follow them. The key is consistency and discipline. Almost anybody can make up a list of rules that are 80% as good as what we taught people. What we couldn't do is give them the confidence to stick to those rules even when things are going bad.
>
> (Quoted in *New Market Wizards*, by Jack Schwager)

In trading you will ultimately have to overcome what is likely to be your own biggest challenge: yourself. Embrace it, it is a part of the journey!

Often when I meet traders they will, at some point, tell me of their discipline challenges. Some of these traders see themselves as being ill-disciplined, and talk at length of their poor discipline. This will in all likelihood merely compound matters, reinforcing their problems with negative self-imaging.

It is important to understand that discipline is a general term, an umbrella for a variety of different trading behaviours, and that very few traders have challenges with *every* one of these behaviours. Indeed in most cases it is one or two areas that are the major obstacles to moving their trading on to the next level.

It is useful for us as traders to be aware of the components of discipline and to be able to specifically define our challenges so that we can seek the required methodology to address them. When a car breaks down it is very rare, if ever, that the whole car fails – it is usually one or two component parts. But some component parts are obviously more important and have a greater impact on overall operation than others when broken; this is the same for us as traders. Isolating your *specific* challenges will help you target and defeat them, as well as keeping your discipline difficulties in perspective.

So when do traders lose discipline?

Reasons Why Traders Lose Discipline

"Investing is not a game where the guy with the 160 IQ beats the guy with the 130 IQ... Once you have ordinary intelligence, what you need is the temperament to control the urges that get other people into trouble in investing."
– Warren Buffett

There follows a list of times and events where traders are prone to losing their discipline. I have broken them down into five core headings; strategy, mental, emotional/psychological, situational and personality.

1. Strategy

- Not having a clearly defined strategy with an edge is the first typical problem here. Having this is a pre-requisite to successful, consistent, disciplined trading. Without one it is actually impossible to see if you are being disciplined or not, as there is no accountability as to whether you followed your plan and stuck to your strategy – not having had one in the first place! Without having clearly defined trading opportunities, you are trading in a more random and haphazard fashion, which will quickly lead, if not there already, to dangerous ill-discipline. Trading a time frame, style or market that does not match your talents, skills, risk tolerance, personality or interests is another problem. If you are trading in a way that is not best suited to you, and particularly if this is a long way off-course, then cracks will appear and elements of ill-discipline will occur. This isn't a problem with yourself as a trader, but arises simply because you and your strategy are out of line. For example, someone who is trading a short time frame, but who is a much more analytical and slower thinker and decision-maker, may find that they have challenges in taking trades with sufficient speed. To make matters worse, they then get frustrated that they missed out, and end up getting in too late and chasing the trade.

> **❝** With no strategy, you can never gauge discipline, or, truly, success. **❞**

- Loss of confidence in trading strategy; lack of understanding of probability and statistics. Sometimes you will get a run of losing trades for no other reason than the fact that you are trading in an environment that contains randomness (the market) and you will not know the distribution of the outcomes of your strategy. Losing streaks are not uncommon or unnatural. If you toss a coin one hundred times you will get at least four strings of either four heads or tails in a row, and potentially you can get five, six or more in a row. When you understand this, coping with a string of losses is easier; and the temptation to try and recklessly recover them is lessened.

2. Mental

- Environmental/external distractions and quiet times in markets – or just plain boredom – is the first mental issue. One of the biggest revelations that many new traders experience is that trading is not a 100% full-on, adrenaline-fuelled rollercoaster! There are often long periods where not much is happening, and the markets are quiet. The danger here is that you get bored and trade just to do something, and not because a trading opportunity as defined by your strategy has arisen. Ask yourself – are you trading to relieve boredom or to make money? Find other tasks to do while the markets are quiet – reading, research, strategy development and so on.

- Fatigue and mental overload lead to poor concentration. As well as being quiet, trading can equally have very long hours and the intensity levels can be exceptionally high. Traders after a long day in the markets can feel mentally and physically tired. As you begin to tire, your risk of error is greatly increased (hence the tight working hour controls placed on people in safety critical environments) and your performance levels will decline. Firstly, ensure that you are managing your physical energy to counter this decline. And secondly, monitor your energy levels throughout the day so that you can be aware and respond accordingly should they go beyond your desired level for good performance.

3. Emotional/Psychological

- Anger and frustration following losses/poor trading can be dangerous. The changes that occur to your physiology and psychology when you are angry and frustrated affect your ability to make objective and reasoned decisions. You are greatly at risk of trading emotionally and *not* objectively. Take time out and wait until you are in a good trading state before re-entering the markets.

- Overconfidence resulting from a string of successes is the flipside risk. Overconfidence is a dangerous feeling – it will get you involved in the markets and with bigger positions than might be appropriate! Create awareness of when overconfidence might occur for you; and, where necessary, stop trading, or consciously manage your positions.

- Unwillingness to accept losses (loss aversion/ego) is a common problem. If you are not willing to take a loss then you are always likely to run one and to move stops. Accepting losses and dealing with them effectively is key to disciplined trading.

- Taking on too much risk. High risk creates higher stress, and higher stress creates stronger anxiety and worry; all this weighs down badly on your decision-making ability. Excessive positions also carry with them the potential for huge painful losses that no one wants to take. So taking *appropriate* risk is a key necessity of, as well as component in, disciplined trading.

- Greed is another pitfall. Wanting too much too soon, or trying to make every trade a big winner, are common. Again the key is to assess your strategy, accept that as traders we are in and out of the market over our desired time frame, whilst the market moves both before and after we enter and exit. Our aim is to capture profits within the time frame of our system.

- Fear. This can come in many forms and may lead to you either not entering the market or getting out too late or too early. Fear of loss, fear of missing out, fear of leaving money on the table are just three possibilities. Managing trading position size, accepting losses as a part of trading, and having confidence in your trading strategy and your own trading ability will all help to reduce or eliminate any fears.

4. Situational

- Situational pressures – slumps, financial pressures, stress outside of trading. Sometimes trading does not go to plan or you get a period of drawdown that might be extended in time or deep in cost. Likewise, sometimes life outside of trading presents challenges that can have an impact on you. Where these conditions arise, your mindset can often be affected; and, as a result, your behaviours can become less disciplined. A typical example is where traders are having financial difficulties either in their trading or outside of work and they start to get into desperation-mode. Their only goal becomes to make money in any way possible, which immediately moves them away from the discipline of sticking to their strategy.

5. Personality

- Some people are by nature not rule-driven, and may live rather by the rebellious axiom that 'rules are there to be broken'. Others may be impulsive, whilst still others may be sensation-seekers who love excitement and high level risk-taking. In all of these cases there is a potential challenge to discipline, so the key issues become getting the best match of the trader to a trading style that most accommodates their personality and/or working with them to make some changes in their natural approach (the second of these is by far the hardest, especially if the behaviours are well ingrained).

"Face your deficiencies and acknowledge them. But do not let them master you."

– Helen Keller

Go through the aforementioned list and identify your trading strengths.

Now go through and identify your weaknesses – your dark side! – consider the frequency of which these events occur and the magnitude of them (the impact) and then rank them in order of priority to address.

What do you need to do to work on these?

You will find many of these dark side behaviours and their possible solutions in the rest of Part Two.

Ideal Trading State

I have heard many people say that they would like to trade with no emotion – would you? If you said yes, then hopefully I will persuade to change your mind!

I know exactly what they and you mean when they say this, and it is not that they want to have *no* emotion at all. What they are really trying to articulate is that they want to have no 'negative' emotion – fear, anger, greed, etc.

Some states are conducive to peak performance trading and some are not. Some states hinder optimal trading performance from taking place. Trying to do something when you are not in the right state is like putting your foot on the accelerator when the car is not in gear – lots of revs, but you don't go anywhere!

Most people have heard of the phrase 'being in the zone' or 'in the flow'. These are phrases that have been made popular by performance psychologists to describe people who are performing at their peak. When people achieve such states they will have accessed and be in their Ideal Performance State or, in trading terms, Ideal *Trading* State. Getting into your ITS is important because it enables you to fully access your trading talent and to perform to your maximum potential.

When I talk to traders about when they have traded at their very best – when they have had those peak moments – they typically describe them using words such as:

- Physically and mentally relaxed

- Alert

- Feeling in control

- Calm

- Energised

- Positive

- Focussed

- Confident

- Effortless

- Automatic

In *Stress for Success*, James E. Loehr explains that "IPS [Ideal Performance State] is a learnt response and is a highly unique and specific response to stress with a high emotional content. It is linked to underlying physiological and neurological events, and enables you to express your talents and skills to the best of your ability."

Exercise: Assessing Your Trading States

What states do you experience as a trader? How do those states affect your trading performance? What states are useful to you as a trader and what do they enable you to do?

Take a look at the list of states above.

Which of these have you encountered in your trading recently?

What percentage of the time that you trade do you spend in 'useful states' vs. 'limiting states'?

How much better could your trading performance be if you were to spend a greater proportion of your trading time in your ideal trading state?

Identifying Your Ideal Trading State

How are you feeling right now? How do you know?

Every emotion has its own 'signature', its own set of physiological and psychological characteristics. The model below shows the component parts to that signature:

- Environmental factors

- Physical factors

- Cognitive (psychological) factors

Because factors that are environmental are often outside of our immediate control I like to think about states being predominantly the by-product of our physiology and psychology. This empowers you as it provides you with the ability to be able to take control of your states to create peak states by learning to manage your physiology and your cognitive processes. Every state has its own unique signature or blueprint. Once you know the blueprints for any state then you can begin to create them. All you have to do is to think of the state and this helps you to access it.

- How is my physiology in that state? How is my breathing? How is my muscle tension? How is my heart rate?

- How is my body language? Gestures? Facial expression?

- How are my energy levels? Tired? Hungry? Dehydrated?

- What thoughts do I have?

- What images do I have/create?

In going through these questions, you begin to uncover the blueprint of your emotions. Once you know these it gives you a massive power. If you want to activate a particular feeling, you can create it by changing your thinking, images, body language and physiology to those of the signature of the feeling that you would like. Any time you make a change to any component part of a feeling, you will experience a different feeling.

For example, think about anxiety. One of the key parts of the blueprint in anxiety is quicker, shallower, upper thoracic (high in the chest) breathing. If you were feeling anxious, and you noticed this level of breathing, then by slowing your breathing down and by breathing from the diaphragm (stomach area) you would be altering your physiology and so creating a change in state. But, importantly, by changing your breathing in this way, you are now activating a physiological component of being calm, composed and confident.

Gaining an awareness of what you are feeling and how you are creating that feeling is a key part of becoming good at managing your emotions. The next stage is to become skilled (yes, it is a skill, and is developed like any other skill through practice) at changing your states by learning to take control of what and how you are thinking, the images you are creating and your physical factors.

This is what the best performers in any area do to manage their emotions and it is exactly the same way in which actors are able to activate strong and convincing emotional responses when they are performing.

Trade when you are at your best. Many people trade when they are not at their best, *knowing* that they are not at their best. Nothing is worse than when this happens and you lose money, confirming what you already thought – I shouldn't have traded!

Being able to recognise when you are at your best, in your ITS, and to trade when you are in such states – or at least at close as possible – is important to achieving consistency in your performance. When you trade in states that are not conducive to trading it is not that you cannot make money or won't make money, but that the chances of you trading well are reduced; and, importantly, your risk profile has increased – if you are not at your best, then your decision-making ability is reduced, and your risk of poor execution and error is increased.

The next time you trade, as a part of your preparation think about your Ideal Trading State and 'check in' to assess where you are at. If you are in your ITS then great – trade on! If you are not, especially if you are significantly far away from it, then look at the blueprint and review what factors are and are not there. Make the necessary changes and trade when you are more towards your ITS. When it is proving very difficult to change your state and to move towards a more positive one then this is important feedback. It is higher risk to trade in a non-peak state, and so your first priority should be to address the negative state that you are experiencing, and then once you have released these feelings you can activate your ITS and begin trading.

Practical Strategy: Checking In

Before you can do this, you will need to have spent some time identifying your Ideal Trading State (ITS).

Checking in is a simple but very effective act. You simply allocate your ITS a measure of 10 and then give a 1 to the worst possible state you could be in to trade! You now have a scale of 1-10.

Take a moment then to check in – where would you put yourself at this point in time?

Now to make the process more effective when you check in ask yourself these questions:

How am I feeling right now? – scale of 1-10

What is that feeling/those feelings? – identify what you are feeling

How did I know that? – what is the evidence/symptoms?

What can I do to get a higher score and move towards my ITS (where appropriate)?

Checking in is a quick and simple way to assess your current trading state. When should you check in? Good times to check in are:

• As a part of your preparation before trading

• After a significant loss or win

• After a string of winners or losers

- On returning to trading after a break for any reason

- After making an error

- Throughout the afternoon when tiredness and fatigue may become more prevalent

- Whenever you want to assess your state!

STRATEGY 12

Deal With Distraction – Refocussing Strategies

"It's very easy to lose focus; throughout the day, you get emails, phone calls, text messages, letters, etc, all of which have nothing to do with your trading life and can easily distract you. If you see yourself frequently losing focus, you need to establish a ritual to get back into the game. Recall Jonny Wilkinson's ritual preparation before a penalty kick. It might be a simple checklist of procedures that you go through, but it's essential."

– Harold Cataquet, Cataquet and Associates Ltd

Recovery is Key

It is a myth that the best performers have a totally unshakeable focus. All great performers lose focus now and again. What separates out the great from the good is that the great are able to refocus quickly, and with as little disruption to their performance as possible. The same is true with traders.

All traders lose focus and get distracted every now and then – some a lot more than others, and for some it will be much more due to external factors, whilst for others it will be more internal; their own thoughts. The keys are recognising that this has occurred and then refocussing as quickly as possible and getting back into performance mode. It is therefore important as a trader to have a technique or a strategy for refocussing – this might be needed after a loss, a series of losses, making an error/fat finger, returning to your desk, talking with someone, being on the phone, etc.

Dealing Effectively With Distractions

There are many things that can become distractions and there are three performance skills that can be utilised to assist in coping with these.

The most important concept that I can get across to any trader is that, in trying to avoid anything, you are often in fact drawn to it. *Don't think about a pink elephant!* I suspect I would not be wrong in saying that salmon-coloured pachyderms just passed through the minds of most readers.

Take driving as an example of how to avoid this. Are you trying to block out every single possible distraction along the way? You couldn't; in fact, if you tried to, you would probably crash. So what do you do? Well, you pay attention to the factors that are *most important* in driving safely: you look where you are going; you scan the mirrors; you monitor your speed; etc. The distractions then naturally fall by the wayside or are subsumed by, and dealt with in, these other activities. So focussing on the performance-critical factors is key, because in doing so by nature we block out or conquer distractions – we can only focus on a few things at a time. The most important aspect of focus is therefore staying task-focussed, i.e. focussing on what has to be done, and not on the outcome. The key is to stay in the present, the now. To take everything trade-by-trade.

My second point relates to the first in terms of our driving example. Whilst it is important to focus on the performance-critical factors, there are always possible distractions that can take us away from this; and where we can identify these we can look at whether they can be removed or reduced (e.g. phones, internet, emails).

Thirdly, and in fact probably most importantly, is recovery! We are all human and therefore we are all going to get distracted, to lose focus at times. This is perfectly normal. We can attempt to stay focussed on our trading execution and we can manage distractions, but ultimately we will all lapse eventually. The most important factor then becomes how quickly we can recover and regain our focus. Indeed one of the key performance differentiators between the best sports people and the rest, and the best traders and the rest, is not so much in whether they make mistakes or lose focus, but in how quickly they can recover that focus and get back in the game effectively. The next section will cover this.

Practical Strategies: Refocussing

1. Check In

The first step, as in all areas of performance, is to have awareness of when you have lost or are losing focus and concentration. It can be useful to monitor your performance state on a scale of 1-10, where 10 is the ideal trading state, and a 1 is when you are completely distracted and in the wrong frame of mind to trade.

2. Quick Refocus: Performance Cues

If you need a quick refocus, using a performance cue will be sufficient in most cases. A performance cue is simply a word or few words that helps you to direct your focus. Examples of simple performance cues include:

- *Focus*
- *Calm*
- *Keep it simple*
- *Trade-by-trade*
- *Patient and profit*
- *Trade the plan*

3. Present Moment Technique

This technique comes from Jeffrey Hodges and might be, for you, a very quick, simple and powerful way to regain focus:

Stop and focus your attention on factors that are external to you. Look around at what you can see. Become aware of any external sounds. Notice the temperature in the room. Do this for 10 seconds.

Breathe in and out slowly for 10 seconds (could be in for 5 and out for 5).

Spend 10 seconds visualising yourself doing whatever you are going to be doing next well.

I have found this particularly useful when traders are getting distracted by their own thoughts and talk, as it removes you from the immediate confusion. I also believe that it can be a great pre-performance technique for the same reasons.

4. Time-out

Where you notice that you are very distracted/unfocussed, and you are in an un-resourceful performance state, it is advisable to take a 'time-out'. Here is a sample:

Take a time-out and move away from the computer screen. Go for a break.

Review your performance – feedback – learning – action – be objective (imagine watching yourself performing and evaluate it as a coach would do).

Breathing exercise.

Refocus – performance cue/process goals.

Visualise trading successfully/implementing cues/processes.

STRATEGY 13

Stay Calm When the Pressure is On

"Harnessing nerves and feeling the pressure just gets you so focussed and gets your concentration level to where it needs to be. I harness that nervous energy in a positive way."

– Tom Lehman, golfer

Dive, Survive or Thrive

In all high-performance activities there are times when the heat is really on and the pressure is high. These situations can often be referred to as *critical moments* – moments where how you think, feel, behave and therefore perform will have significant consequences.

Great athletes relish these critical moments – the moments that can define a game, that can lead to victory or loss. The kicker in rugby who steps up to take the final penalty kick or drop goal to win the match; the footballers who step-up to take the penalties in the cup final; the golfer who has to make the final putt to win the tournament; the tennis player serving to win a grand slam.

In trading it is the trader who suddenly has to deal with a large trading position in a market that has suddenly become more volatile; the trader who has to cut his position as the market moves quickly against him; the trader who reacts quickly and decisively to enter the market as a good trading opportunity appears; the trader who sticks to his strategy through ups and downs, seeing the trade out to its conclusion; or the trader who makes a mistake that leaves them in an undesirable situation, who then calmly deals with it and gets the best achievable outcome.

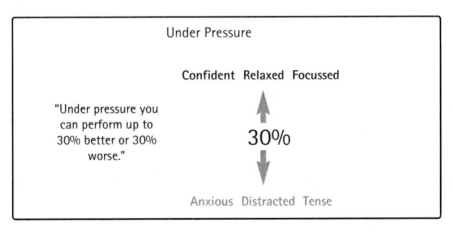

When the pressure is on, there are generally three responses:

1. You dive – you crack under the pressure, called 'choking' in sport, and you under-perform.

2. You survive – you get through.

3. You thrive – you relish the challenge of the opportunity and the pressure raises your performance.

When the pressure is really on what is your response?

Think of some high pressure situations you have encountered, how you reacted to them and how you performed.

Did you dive, survive or thrive?

Don't Choke!

In *The Game Plan* by Steve Bull he talks of how the mention of choking, or cracking under the pressure, is not allowed in many sports teams' changing rooms. Why? In 1988 Professor Larry Leith wrote a paper for the *International Journal of Sports Psychology* entitled 'Choking in Sports: Are We Our Own Worst Enemies?' Leith's hypothesis was that the very thought of choking would be enough to induce it, so he set up an experiment to test his theory out. He took two groups of university students and set them a basketball shooting challenge. Each group was briefed separately about the challenge and were given almost identical sets of instructions – the one difference being that one of the groups was told, just as they were about to perform, that there was a phenomena in sport known as choking, and he explained what it was and the serious negative impact that it had on a person's performance when it occurred. They were then of course advised not to choke. This group performed significantly less well than the other group in the test. It appears that just the *thought* of choking was enough to bring about a negative change in performance.

So it would seem that a definite key to performing well in these situations is to have a positive performance expectancy and to not be focussed on not choking. I remember hearing a trader at an institution talking out loud to himself in what was obviously a difficult situation and all I could hear was 'don't mess up, don't mess up, come on, don't mess this up'. This is not at all advisable.

A key to performing well in critical moments is to change your focus from not choking or messing up, to the desired outcome that you *do* want! Your thoughts and where you place your attention are vital determinants of performance and no more so than in these critical moments.

Slow Down: Relax!

When you are really feeling the pressure there is a natural tendency to speed up, to rush. You tend to think quickly, move quickly, breathe more quickly and even talk more quickly; and time itself appears to quicken. These are physical changes that are occurring in response to your change in state. These physical changes are not conducive to helping you perform well under pressure, and so a really important strategy for helping you to deal with pressure moments more effectively is to slow down – to breathe more slowly, move more slowly, talk and think more slowly. You may be very surprised by just how significantly this simple technique helps to keep you more composed and gives you a sense of control and of confidence.

Deep breathing is also a very powerful tool for calming you down.

Exercise: Critical Moment Deep Breathing

Slowly inhale through your nose, breathing in from your diaphragm (belly) – imagine inflating a large balloon in your stomach – and then filling your lungs from the bottom to the top. I like to use a five second count – if you find this uncomfortable then find your own rhythm.

Breathe out through your mouth for five seconds (or your own rhythm – but equal to the in-breath) letting the air go from the top of the lungs down to your diaphragm.

Repeat.

With practice it may be that over time you will find just one or two cycles of this can have a significant impact on how you feel – eventually your deep breathing will become a trigger, a switch to activate your calmer and more composed state.

Exercise: Centering

Centring is a simple technique that you can use to control stress and muscle tension, block out negative or distracting thoughts, and refocus your attention on task-relevant cues.

Sit in a comfortable and upright position. Legs and arms unfolded/uncrossed.

Take a deep breath in from the abdomen, and imagine the air circulating around the body.

Exhale slowly and completely, and as you do so feel your neck and shoulders relaxing, and this relaxation spreading through the rest of the body.

As you finish the breath, think about the single most important component to focus on right now – performance cue.

See Success

Critical moments in trading are sometimes totally unforeseen and unexpected. However, for the most part, although we do not know when they will appear, we do know the nature of them – we know the types of events that occur. Because of this it means that we can prepare ourselves for dealing with them.

List the events that are likely to occur and write down specifically what you will do in each situation. Reading through these and becoming familiar with them can help you to react more effectively in the heat of the moment.

Utilise mental rehearsal to see yourself responding in a cool, calm and collected fashion in those moments. Notice what you see, hear and feel as you deal with the situation. By doing this you are creating the specific neurology within the brain to enable you to perform that way in a more automatic and natural way when the events arise.

Knowing that you are prepared for such events can help you to feel more in control, and, importantly, more confident when they happen.

Experience is a Great Teacher

Over time you will build up a great deal of experience as a trader, trading a whole host of different market conditions and encountering many critical moments. Each time you are put on the line you will dive, survive or thrive! Each moment will give you specific feedback about how you dealt with the situation, what you did well, what you could improve on, and what action you can take in the future to be even more effective.

I remember working with a trader who had traded through a wide variety of difficult market conditions over his extensive career, including the Asian crisis and the 1987 stock market crash. His view was that these experiences had strengthened him as a trader; even to the extent that he now perceived himself to be a great crisis trader – a person who relished conditions away from the norm, who loved the critical moments that trading can bring!

Are You a Critical Moment Performer?

"You cannot outperform your self-image."

– Dennis Connor, Americas Cup skipper

How you see yourself (your self-image) has a big impact on how you perform. Do you see yourself as someone who chokes under pressure? If so, guess what is going to happen! Do you see yourself as someone who is cool and calm under pressure? If so, guess what is going to happen! We arguably perform in line with our self-image – our self-held reality of who we are and how we do things. Our self-image is essentially a collection of beliefs about what we think to be true about ourselves and can be developed and conditioned through building empowering beliefs and positive self-talk.

Real Life Example: Coping With Critical Moments

Samir was a trader who thrived on trading big economic data and events where the markets moved fast and the pressure was high with big trading positions.

I asked him if he did anything to help him to perform so well in these particular situations, and he told me he did the following:

"Thorough preparation before each release/event, including writing a strategy for how I will trade it, looking at all the possible 'what if?' scenarios and deciding what I would do in each one, and then using mental rehearsal to see myself carrying out my plan and different approaches.

"I use deep breathing and 'meditation' regularly and before any key events, and sometimes during them. I find that by spending time on controlling my breathing I am able to stay more in control when things get tight.

"I believe that I will trade well and that I will make money more often than not. I guess I have recognised trading these events as a strength and my results give me the confidence to trade them with good size and conviction. If things go wrong or I get caught I have enough experience to generally work something out, or if I get really caught then I just have to take the loss."

Practical Strategy: Developing Critical Moment Peak Performance

Identify as many specific critical moments as you can.

Where possible, develop the skills and abilities that will help you to perform well in these situations. Competence is key to confidence. Knowing that you have what it takes to deal with these moments will be significant in how well you perform.

Focus only on those aspects of performance that are under your control. Identify these for any possible critical moment and then focus on them

Slow down! Slow down your breathing, speed of movement, how quickly you are talking and thinking.

Mentally rehearse being in specific critical moment situations – see yourself staying cool, calm and collected, and performing well.

Learn from every critical moment that you encounter, build your knowledge bank and your level of experience, and utilise these to improve your performance in the future.

STRATEGY 14

Get Energised – Manage Your Energy Levels

"Fatigue makes cowards of us all!"

– Vince Lombardi, American Football coaching legend

Energy is Critical to Peak Performance

Physical energy is one of the foundations of peak performance. Yes, you need the appropriate technique and ability to master your craft. Yes, you need to spend regular and systematic time researching fundamentals and honing your technical skills. But your ability to translate the talent you have as a trader into an engaged performance rests not only on skill but on your ability to manage energy.

Energy management takes place on a macro scale in terms of exercise, diet, rest, relaxation and sleep, and also on a micro scale – throughout the trading day, particularly as regards nutrition and rest/recovery.

In physical training, getting fitter, stronger, more skilful, faster and so on all requires appropriate periods of training, with sufficient rest and recovery – a period known as overcompensation – for the required growth to occur. This is equally true for your trading performance where you want to balance periods of full engagement with periods of active disengagement – quality recovery. Getting this balance will maintain your performance at *higher* levels for *greater* periods of time.

Exercise: Energy Management Reflection

How would you describe your energy state right now? 0 (low) – 10 (high)

Can you remember a time when you had really high energy? What was that like? How was your performance level?

Can you remember a time when you were really low in energy? How did that affect your performance?

Real Life Example: Declining Concentration and Poor Performance in the Afternoon

I remember coaching a trader once who was having challenges in his trading. He was trading well in the morning but his afternoon trading session was littered with lapses in concentration, errors and a marked increase in emotional outbursts. From his perspective the markets and his trading strategy did not change dramatically from one session to the other, and so his concern was his inability to maintain his focus during the afternoon.

This sounded like a typical energy level issue, so I asked him about his lifestyle. His sleep was 5 hours on average a night; his diet was packed with junk food and high refined sugar products; he drank a lot of coffee but little water and exercised very infrequently (in fact, hardly ever).

The coaching outcome we aimed for was to improve focus in the afternoons, to enhance concentration and reduce errors and poor decisions. The intervention included aiming for a minimum of 6 hours sleep every night; some dietary changes, including eating more whole grain products and reducing the number of sugary snacks consumed; replacing every other cup of coffee with a glass of water; and building in some walking and a weekly session of squash (a game which he played on occasions and really enjoyed).

> **Within two weeks of following new pro-energy routines, his afternoon trading had radically improved.**

Within the first two weeks he could already feel the difference, and after four weeks his afternoon trading had taken a huge turn for the better. His concentration had dramatically improved and he was making hardly any errors.

The Importance of Energy

Your energy levels play a big part in your trading performance as they affect your mood, sensitivity to mood change, your concentration and focus, stress levels, reaction speed and cognitive processing ability. All of these are fundamental components of high-performance trading.

Imagine your energy levels as a bank account: if you consistently withdraw energy without depositing any, your reserves will run out, leading to reduced performance over time.

The trading arena is prone to intense adversities and stresses, and therefore demands greater amounts of energy.

Managing Physical Energy

One of the key strategies for keeping your energy account high is to build on and maintain a high 'energy platform'. As the section below shows, this platform consists of nutrition, exercise, rest/relaxation and sleep – NERS.

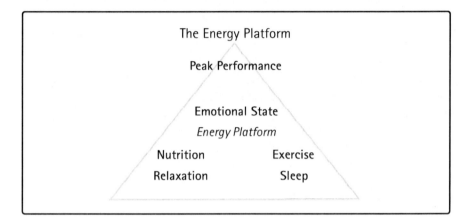

The Energy Platform

Peak Performance

Emotional State

Energy Platform

Nutrition   Exercise

Relaxation   Sleep

Key factors in a strong energy base

- Nutrition: Balanced diet; low sugar/salt; fruit/veg/grains etc. Plenty of water.
- Exercise: Balance of cardio and weights (3:2). 5 x 30 minutes per week.
- Rest/Relaxation: Time to switch off, do activities for fun, downtime.
- Sleep: 6-8 hours per night.

(Based on guidelines from *The Power of Full Engagement* by James E. Loehr and Tony Schwartz.)

N.B. These are guidelines only and each individual should seek appropriate medical or professional advice before making any significant dietary changes or taking up increased physical activity.

Brain smart nutrition

Trading is a cognitive process and peak performance requires optimal brain functioning. Nutrition has a big impact on your level of brain functioning and on your trading performance. Here are a few key tips based on research conducted by the USDA (United States Department of Agriculture).

Make breakfast happen

Skipping breakfast, which is the most important meal of the day, can impact negatively on your memory and cognitive skills. Going all night without food and then skipping breakfast may cause your blood sugar levels to dip, causing less sugar in the form of glucose – the brain's primary source of fuel – to get to the brain.

Stay hydrated

Between 55% and 60% of your body, and more than 70% of your brain, is composed of water. If your brain hydration dips below this level it impacts on performance in the forms of headaches, and feeling slower and less sharp. Make sure you drink plenty of water during the day and be extra careful if you are working in air-conditioned environments; the dry indoor air can accelerate fluid loss.

Lighten up at lunch

You have probably experienced the sleepy after-effects of a big heavy lunch before! This is caused by the digestive tract diverting blood away from other parts of your body, leaving you feeling tired and sluggish. Studies show that a meal of greater than 1000 calories at midday can cause more drowsiness than lunches half that size.

Snack intelligently

If you feel tired or hungry, eat a small light snack – raisins are great, as they contain boron, which combats drowsiness; brazil nuts have selenium which lifts your mood and can help you to feel clearheaded; fruit or crunchy vegetables are a great source of carbohydrate for energy.

Oscillation – Balancing Stress and Recovery

"Consistent performance is achieved when you have a healthy oscillation between positive peak performance states, and periods of recovery."

– James E. Loehr, *Stress for Success*

Seeking regular and valuable recovery throughout our practice as traders renews our energy, and allows us to become more fully engaged in what we are doing.

As part of this, it is important to take regular breaks. James E. Loehr in *Stress for Success* suggests taking breaks and eating and drinking approximately every 2 hours, in order to regulate and stabilise the body's energy levels and metabolism.

Ernest Rossi suggests the body and mind work on an ultradian rhythm. This is a naturally occurring, although often suppressed, rhythm taking place on a cycle of 90 minutes +/- of peak focus/energy, followed by a natural recovery dip of 15/20 minutes +/-.

The dip is often signalled to us by factors such as hunger pangs, yawning, daydreaming and loss of concentration. It is the mind's natural idling time, and enables the unconscious to process information and integrate learning. By denying breaks, although often with positive intention, we end up with subsequently lower and lower peaks – hence the feeling of declining energy and concentration throughout the day. To combat this, use the following REFS ritual.

Combat declining energy and concentration by taking REFS

Rest/Relax: Get away from the screen (rest eyes/mind/body)

Eat: Have something healthy to eat

Fluids: Drink water/juice etc

Stretch: Get up, move around, go for a walk, get the muscles moving

Practical Strategy: Top Three Tips for Managing Energy

The key to energy management lies in the creation of positive routines and rituals.

1. Increasing your awareness of your ongoing states is the first step to optimal energy management. Check in on a 1 – 10 scale regularly throughout the day, and over time. N.B. Long periods of feeling tired, frustrated, angry, depressed, unmotivated, etc, strongly indicate an imbalance, and a need for action.

2. Build a strong energy platform through good nutrition, regular exercise, good quality and quantity of sleep, and getting plenty of rest and recovery – NERS.

3. Use the concept of oscillation – balancing periods of stress with periods of recovery – to maintain energy and the ability to access peak performance states – REFS.

STRATEGY 15

Run Your Profits, Cut Your Losses

"When I was younger, my father used to always talk to me and my brother (now a trader too) about gambling and, more specifically, gamblers. He would always say that 'it is far easier to train an elite Special Forces soldier than it is to train a successful professional gambler'. This was because he felt that our inherent human weaknesses in respect of containing the parameters of our betting, and in deciding when we should stop and when we should continue betting, are extremely difficult to control. The evidence of which, if any were really needed, can be found in the profits of a roulette table over a long period of time, as the figure would almost surely outweigh that which may be calculated through the use of the 'house edge'."

– Edward Arees, trader

The Golden Rule!

Ithink that you would be hard pressed to find any trader who did not know the golden rule of trading: 'Run your profits, cut your losses.' We all know at a conceptual and rational level that this makes sense, and is indeed key to long-term profitability.

But if this is the case, then why is it that so many people not only do not do this, but actually do the exact opposite – and run losses whilst cutting profits!

Reflect on your own trading – how is your risk and money management in your trades? How frequently do you run losses? How frequently do you cut profits?

A great calculation to make is to work out your average winning trade and then work out your average losing trade. Now divide the average winning trade by the average losing trade, and this will give you a figure that is called the pay-off ratio and is indicative of your risk:reward levels.

Pay-off Ratio – Indicator of Risk:Reward

Trader John

Average Winning Trade $3000

Average Losing Trade $5000

Pay-off Ratio $3000/$5000 = 0.6.

A figure of 1 would indicate a 1:1 ratio. Greater than 1 and you are making more when you win, than you lose when you lose; less than 1 and your losses are greater than your wins.

You are only human!

It has been mentioned in this book that trading is simple, not easy. Nothing illustrates this point more than people not being able to run profits and cut losses. We have already established that this concept makes sense both intellectually and financially and yet we know that traders still do the opposite. How can that be?

Let's look at some of the reasons why traders run losses and cut profits.

Read the following and then for each choose either option A or B. Take the exercise as seriously as is possible, as if you actually had the money in your hand, and you will get the most from it.

Imagine that you have just been given £1000 and you have been asked to choose between two options. With option A, you are guaranteed to win an additional £500. With option B, you are given the chance to flip a coin. If it is heads you win another £1000; tails, you get nothing more. Which would you choose?

Now imagine you have just been given £2000 and are required to choose between two options. With option A, you are guaranteed to lose £500. With option B, you are given the chance to flip a coin. If it's heads, you lose £1000; tails you lose nothing. Which option would you choose?

What did you do? If you went for option A in the first one, then you are with the majority of people who have been asked this question. You have taken the guaranteed additional £500 instead of taking the additional risk of flipping the coin.

If you went for option B in the second one, then you would have again been in the majority of people. You chose to take additional risk in a situation of loss rather than to take the guaranteed one.

Now let's look at this in trading terms. If you took option A in the first scenario then you essentially chose to guarantee your return when in a situation of gain, rather than choosing to take additional risk, which is what the people who chose B have done. In trading terms, you have cut your winner.

If you went for option B in the second scenario, then you have chosen to take additional risk or in trading terms you have run your loss.

The research done in behavioural finance suggests that the majority of people in a situation of gain will become risk averse (take less risk); whilst in a situation of loss they are more likely to become risk-taking. In trading terms, the majority of people when in a winning position are likely to cut the winner, whilst in a situation of loss they are likely to run the loss.

The significance of this is great, as it is essentially suggesting that the majority of people will have natural instincts – a psychological bias – towards behaviours that are the opposite of what is required to become successful in trading. Meanwhile, only a small number of people may possess the natural instincts to think in the ways and act in the ways that allow them to not only rationalise the idea of running profits and cutting losses, but be able to actualise it too!

Is this doom and gloom for the majority then? Well, maybe; and perhaps it is a factor in why so few traders achieve and sustain success. But I feel this is not totally the case, although it does mean that trading success will take time and effort because you will have to recondition and train yourself to overcome your natural instincts or "urges", as Warren Buffet calls them.

You May Need to Learn to Think, Feel and Behave Differently

Exercise – Re-Conditioning

Fold your arms.

Notice your own unique style. Where are your hands placed? How are your fingers spaced? How much tension is there in your muscles? Which arm crosses over which?

Now fold your arms again but in completely the opposite way!

How did that feel?

Probably awkward and uncomfortable, unnatural, not instinctive?

How would you go about learning to fold your arms the other way around?

Practise, practise and practise! You have to recondition your new response. This is exactly the process required for changing your mindset with profits and losses.

"The three elements of successful trading are: Cutting losses, cutting losses, cutting losses. If you can follow these rules, you may have a chance!"

– Ed Seykota in *Market Wizards*

It is important to accept the fact that it is likely, statistically, that you may have to recondition and overcome your natural instincts on this point. Understanding that this is a part of becoming a trader is important. It is not just your trading skills and knowledge that you need to develop, but also your psychological skills and abilities too. Accepting this, preparing for it and being proactive in working on it, will all help to stack the odds of success that little more in your favour!

However, there are also other factors that come into play when it comes to running losses and cutting profits, or ideally, achieving the opposite!

Taking a loss or running a profit is also not easy psychologically because:

- We don't like to lose! Culturally high percentages are related to being successful and taking a loss costs us money and affects our win/loss ratio! On the flipside, when our trading positions are onside in a profitable position then taking that profit adds to our win:loss ratio, and our percentage success rate is increased.

- Ego! Your ego functions around the central objectives of looking good and being right. Taking a loss can be seen as being wrong and is therefore a dent to one's ego, whilst taking a profit confirms that you were right and is an ego-positive.

What also really interests me is why so many traders seek to compound this situation and make it *even harder* to take a loss or run profits.

How do they do this?

1. *Taking excessive risk in relation to their trading account.* When you take excessive risk in relation to your trading account, you are creating a higher level of mental engagement and stress, which impacts upon your decision-making.

   The financial swings of each price movement are so great that they release adrenaline into your system, and whilst this trading may be exciting, the end-result is that often the trader snatches profits as soon as they can to avoid large swings into negative P&L territory, or if they are already in that territory they hang on and hope that the market comes back to avoid them having to take a big loss.

I like to encourage traders to think about the relationship between trading account size and position sizing, and for those traders trading their own accounts to also consider their trading capital against their personal wealth. If your trading positions are a significant proportion of your trading capital then any given loss is also a big loss of your trading capital – a big double whammy! If your trading capital is also a large proportion of your personal wealth then you have a big triple whammy occurring and that is not a pleasant experience for anyone.

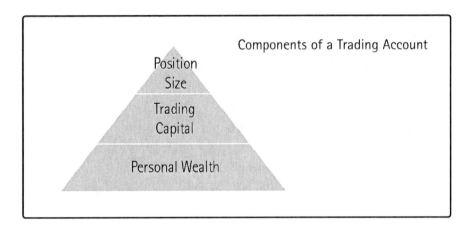

Components of a Trading Account

Position Size

Trading Capital

Personal Wealth

2. *Placing stops at levels where the financial cost of executing the stop is not comfortable.* If you are only comfortable losing £1000 on a trade, and a stop puts you in a situation where the loss would be £2000, what do you think will happen? It is going to be difficult to take a loss that you are not comfortable with! As a part of your trading strategy, you need to consider where your stop needs to be from a strategic perspective, but also from a financial and psychological viewpoint. The challenge is to then size your position to allow each perspective's goals to be achieved.

Real Life Example: Running Losses

I worked with a trader once who came to me because he was having problems with adhering to his intra-day trading stops. He was an experienced and successful trader but felt that he was not trading to his potential because of the excessive losses he was taking.

His intra-day stop was set to £3500 and yet interestingly his typical realised losses were significantly greater than this, being anywhere between £6000 and £30,000. When I talked with him about this finding, it transpired that he was not happy to take a loss of more than £3500 and so often waited to see if the market would come back and 'save' him. On those occasions when it didn't, he was left in a kind of no man's land at the mercy of the market and would eventually cut his position when either rationality set in or the pain of the accrued loss became too great.

When I asked the trader how much money he would feel comfortable losing in a day, he replied, "£2500." That is a full £1000 less than where he had set his stop, or about 30% less! Having his stop at £3500 was putting him into a difficult, and in fact almost a no-win situation, because it was already beyond his comfort threshold.

By adjusting his position sizing he was able to work to a £2500 stop, which proved far more effective and less stressful for him.

3. *Not fully accepting losses as a part of trading.* At a deep level you have to internalise that taking a loss is a natural part of trading, and get to the level where the thought of a loss itself is not an issue for you. Mark Douglas in *Trading in the Zone* suggests that until a trader gets to this stage he will not be able to truly enter the zone state or trade to his potential.

4. *Not having stops or profit targets in the first place.* This makes defining where to get out difficult and more discretionary. So on the downside it is easy to keep moving the stop as price moves, after all 'it could come back!', and on the upside you have no idea where price may go so any tick above zero is potentially a profit taking opportunity. Of course different traders have different styles and the use of stops and targets is a much talked about topic and there is no one solution. However, from a risk and money management perspective, and from a psychological viewpoint, they can be very useful.

"Always have a two-way exit strategy; know when you plan to cut your profits, as well as when to cut your losses. These can be revised frequently, but always refer back to the initial plan to keep that sense of perspective."

– Harold Cataquet, Cataquet and Associates Ltd

5. *Trading when you need to make money.* Desperation is one of the most destructive states that you can trade in. I have, unfortunately, seen many

traders lose their trading accounts due to trading in this mindset. When a trader is desperate to make money any time a trade ticks into profit becomes a chance to bank something, and so profits are cut short. Every time a trade moves offside and towards their stop, the trader cannot mentally afford to take that loss, so they often hang on, hoping and wishing for the market to come back and save them.

 Trader Top Tips

"Failure to stick to money management rules and stops, frequently has disastrous results."

– Stewart Hampton, trader

"Don't get emotionally attached to your trades. You're going to have losing ones, and expecting every one to make you rich means it's that much harder to cut your losses when required."

– Ruban Rajendran, oil trader

Practical Strategy: Making it Easier to Run Profits and Cut Losses

If you are having a challenge in taking a loss or executing a stop then have a look at the five points we've just gone through, and see if you are compounding the situation in any way. If you are not, then you may simply be in the early stages of becoming a trader, and a part of that process is conditioning new attitudes and developing a trader's mindset, learning to think and behave like a successful trader – which is covered elsewhere, so don't worry!

STRATEGY 16

Handle Losses Like a Winner

"I once had the pleasure of sitting next to Luke Donald at a dinner. Many of you won't know Luke, but he was at the time no. 9 on the world golfing ranking list. Of course most of us only know no. 1, Tiger Woods. We forget that Tiger is often challenged to the finish line, and wins by only one or two strokes. Luke is one of those guys who are up there, breathing down Tiger's neck. I asked him who the better golfer was: him or Tiger? Without a moment of hesitation he said: I am the better golfer, but Tiger has a better mental framework. He went on to say that what made Tiger so amazing (apart from his unquestionable golf skills) was that he could play the next hole as if whatever came before had never happened. No matter how poorly he had played the previous hole, it didn't seem to affect him."

— Tom Hougaard

Losses Are a Part of Trading

C an you name a great trader who has never had a losing trade? Losses are a part of trading. I remember hearing Van Tharp say that a loss is to trading what breathing out is to the breathing cycle.

It is not unusual for new traders to have difficulties in taking losses. After all, losing is not something to be desired in most areas of life, so why in trading? We are generally conditioned culturally to aim for very high percentage success rates; in exams, high percentage scores are required to achieve the best grades. But in trading you could be very profitable with a 40% winning percentage; indeed, you could even be amongst the top earning traders. There are not many exams where you can get top marks with 40%.

Taking a loss is not something to be aimed for or enjoyed but at some level you need to accept the fact that losses are a part of trading. And only once you accept the fact that losses are an inevitable part of trading will you be able to trade freely and without fear.

Learning to Take a Loss

"Good trading is not about being right, it is about trading right. If you want to be successful, you need to think of the long run, and ignore the outcome of individual trades."

– Curtis Faith, *Way of the Turtle*

There are lots of different strategies and approaches that you can use to help you to take and deal with losses more effectively. Ultimately your beliefs and attitudes around what a loss means will have the biggest impact to you. I remember working with one trader who saw a loss as a failure, a setback and a waste, and combined with his perfectionist tendencies this made taking any kind of loss a real challenge, and emotionally quite painful and difficult.

But once he had challenged those old beliefs and made the decision to see losses as being a part of the trading experience – something to learn from – and had made the distinction between a losing trade and a bad trade, then his ability to take losses, and to deal with them, dramatically improved.

 ## Trader Top Tips

"Resilience is essential; again it isn't so much how well you deal with success in trading it is how you deal with problems (and there will be a lot of them). When I trade it isn't the financial side of the loss I find difficult, it is when the trade proves to be right and you have paid up or down which is the biggest frustration. I would advise, as I am starting to learn now, you are better just to forget about it and move on – there is always another day."

– Lawrie Inman, trader

"Dealing with losses can be hard. Try to analyse them in an objective way. Working out what went wrong will help you to feel that you have the power to prevent it next time. This will give you the belief that you have come through a better trader, and this will help greatly with the healing process."

– Stewart Hampton, trader

"To always remember to step back and look at the big picture, where the decisions of a current trading day, or even a trading month, are merely a fragment of an overall plan of action. In that way, the trader's bankroll can be managed effectively, the psychological effect of losses can be overcome more easily, and the trader would find less need to gamble for the one big trade, when he/she is aware of the positive effect of consistent accumulation."

– Edward Arees, trader

"I think one of my strengths is that I view anything that has happened up to this point to be history. I really don't care about the mistakes I made three seconds ago in the market. What I care about is what I am going to do from the next moment on."

– Paul Tudor-Jones (in *Market Wizards*)

Practical Strategies: How Do Winners Handle Losses?

Here are a few hints and tips that, if you apply them, will help you to develop your resilience, to deal with losses and setbacks, and to bounce back more quickly.

Develop positive beliefs around losses

Accept that losses are a part of trading, and that setbacks and challenges are a part of achieving any challenging goal. Embrace the challenge. Tiger Woods famously said, "I smile at obstacles".

Keep perspective

Imagine the number of trades that you make in a year and put a single loss into the context of the total number of trades. Imagine someone making 5 trades a day, 25 a week, 100 per month, and over 1000 a year; each trade, a losing trade, as a percentage of those trades is just 0.001%!

Learn and move on

Know that every trade, every loss, every mistake, every setback has something valuable in it... LEARNING! Learn from your losses, mistakes, errors, setbacks. Ask yourself, what have I learnt from that experience? How will I use it to make me a better trader? There is no failure, only feedback, and feedback is the breakfast of champions. Taking learning from losses and setbacks helps to release the emotional attachment to the event – you have acted on the feedback, and can now move forward more easily. See the implementation of the learning from the loss as an investment in your future trading career!

Take a third person perspective when evaluating your losses

Imagine watching yourself trading on a screen, or imagine standing behind yourself as you replay and evaluate your losses. This helps you to evaluate and identify the key areas for improvement, whilst at the same time removing the emotion of replaying the events again.

Don't let a losing trade become *I am a loser*

Refuse to let your losses define you as a person. Separate out the behaviour from you, the person.

Separate a bad trade from a losing trade. What is the difference? A losing trade is one in which you traded your strategy, stuck to the rules and were disciplined, and yet had a negative P&L as the outcome. A bad trade is a trade that was a *non-strategy trade*, and is a bad trade regardless of whether you made or lost money!

Develop a post-loss ritual

ARIA, for example. In his book *Sportsmind*, Jeffrey Hodges outlines a visualisation process for dealing with setbacks and errors which I have used extensively and with great success with traders when they have encountered a loss or series of losses that impacts on their performance.

ARIA – Handling Losing Trades Strategy

Acknowledge in a low-key way that the losing trade was not what you wanted/expected

Release; note the feedback and learning and 'throw' the trade away (almost physically)

Imprint or mentally rehearse what you wish had happened (x 2)

Affirm *that's how I will do it next time*

STRATEGY 17

Parking Errors – Dealing Effectively With Mistakes

"Clumsy typing cost a Japanese bank at least £128 million and staff their Christmas bonuses yesterday, after a trader mistakenly sold 600,000 more shares than he should have.

The trader at Mizuho Securities, who has not been named, fell foul of what is known in financial circles as "fat finger syndrome" where a dealer types incorrect details into his computer. He wanted to sell one share in a new telecoms company called J Com, for 600,000 yen (about £3000).

Unfortunately, the order went through as a sale of 600,000 shares at 1 yen each.

That error alone would have been bad enough, but the consequences were much worse because 600,000 shares represents more than 40 times the total number issued by the company, and the vast discrepancy effectively created a technical shortage of shares, worth about £1.6 billion."

– Times Online, 9 December 2005

Fat Fingers

Have you ever fat-fingered or made an execution error? Chances are you have, if you have been trading long enough – but hopefully nowhere near the scale of the aforementioned Japanese trader (obviously an extreme example!). How did you feel afterwards? I suppose it depends on the result; some traders have fat-fingered and made profit as a result, whilst most have made a loss.

Fat fingers are essentially an execution error caused through keyboard or mouse operation. They are frustrating, because they are avoidable.

Fat fingers can occur through a number of things, including:

- Mental fatigue

- Poor concentration/getting distracted

- Not being prepared and ready

- Poor keyboard/mouse skills

- Lack of practice in execution skills, especially for newer traders

It is important to realise that errors and mistakes will happen, and it is going to be down to *how you deal with them* that defines you as a trader. When you are beginning your journey as a trader it is natural to want to do well and to avoid making mistakes. This can, however, have the effect of making you very tentative and tense, and you end up trading less and getting less market exposure, which simply slows down your learning process. Errors are an integral part of the learning process and need to be, in a sense, embraced by beginners.

"The individual who is mistake-free is also probably sitting around doing nothing. And that is a mistake!"

– John Wooden, legendary NCAA basketball coach

Exercise: Reflection

Reflect on an error/fat finger that you have made.

What was the cause of the error?

Was it avoidable? How?

Two Key Approaches

With regards to fat fingers and errors, there are two important variables to consider as traders. The first one is *preventative* measures; the second, *recovery* strategies.

Firstly, you want the risk of error to be low – (cf the strategies on discipline and preparation) and there are several actions that you can take to accomplish this. Secondly, even with good management there is always some possible risk of making an execution error and when this does occur the priority is *recovery*. Your ability to act quickly in the moment of realisation and then to recover back to a positive trading state will be a strong indicator of your composure and resilience as a trader.

Practical Strategies: Dealing With Errors Effectively

1. Prevention Strategies

> "Be an expert in operating to your execution tools and systems. Silly mistakes cause unnecessary anxiety and hits to confidence."
>
> **– A. F., bank trader**

a. Make sure your execution skills are well practised, and that you take time to practise them again should you switch trading platforms. This is a good use of trading simulators! Trading simulators enable you to trade in real-time and to trade your strategy just as you would in reality, with the exception that your orders do not actually go through to the exchange. They enable you to practise effectively and realistically with no financial risk that may come from the range of calculation, decision-making or simple keyboard errors that are typically involved when using new strategies or platforms.

b. Focus on maintaining good energy throughout the day with hydration, nutrition, exercise and sleep. When you are tired, hungry or dehydrated the risk of error increases. (Remember the strategy 'Get Energised'.)

c. Monitor your levels of concentration and focus, and be prepared to stop trading when they fall below your required performance levels. Think traffic lights – green for good, amber for caution and red for danger/stop. If you find that you are continually being distracted or you just cannot sustain your focus, then your risk of error has increased! Staying hydrated is particularly critical here, as there is a correlation between dehydration levels rising and concentration ability declining.

d. Set up your trading environment so that it has minimum possible distractions. Some traders are very easily distracted by the external environment – TV, phones, people, internet, etc. If this is you, then it is important to set your workspace up so that distractions are minimised whilst you are trading.

2. Recovery Strategies

a. Once you have fat-fingered, the first stage is to deal with what has happened as effectively as possible. Staying calm and rational and achieving the best possible outcome is the goal. What has happened cannot be undone, only dealt with. If you notice you are getting anxious and panicking, then focus on your breathing. Slow down the rate of your breathing and aim to breathe from the diaphragm (belly). (Slow your thoughts down. Say to yourself, if it helps, "I am in control." Focus on what you need to do.)

b. After the event, dealing with any feelings of anger, frustration and so on, and getting re-focussed, should be the goal. This is a prime time to be cautious of chasing losses! Below is an error parking or release strategy that I have used with lots of traders to help with overcoming losses and errors, and that, when practised and implemented regularly, can be very powerful in reducing the impact of such events.

STEP 1: Acknowledge what happened – in a low key and objective way, if possible! "It was not what I wanted."

STEP 2: Let go – take out any learning from the experience, and then release it; some traders use a physical gesture to actually throw it away or into the bin.

STEP 3: Imagine what you would do in the same situation again in the future, and affirm to yourself that that is what you will do. "That's how I will do it next time." In other words, rehearse successful execution.

STEP 4: Refocus – get set and ready to trade. Check your emotional state is positive, envision yourself trading well. Settle back into the markets only when you are *ready*.

c. Develop selective amnesia like the great golfer Jack Nicklaus, who claims never to have three putted on the last whole of a tournament. When reminded by a friend of his that he had done this, Nicklaus insisted that he could not remember it!

Other fat fingers of note

- February 2005: A broker tried to sell 15,000 shares in music publisher EMI at 280p, but instead placed an order for 15 million in a transaction worth £41.5 million.

- April 2003: A trader accidentally bought 500,000 shares in GlaxoSmithKline, the pharmaceuticals group, at £13.00 each when the market price was 70p less.

- November 2002: A market maker confused the price of Ryanair shares in euros and sterling, sending the London quote up more than 61%, from 404.5p to 653.7p.

- October 2002: A keyboard error at Eurex, the world's largest derivatives market, halted trade for three hours and caused its index to fall 500 points after an unidentified London trader entered the wrong price during a futures transaction.

- September 2002: A Eurex trader intended to sell one futures contract when the DAX, Germany's index of leading shares, reached 5180. Instead he sold 5180 contracts, sending the market into a free fall. Five hours later the exchange announced the cancellation of a raft of other trades.

- December 2001: A trader at UBS Warburg, the Swiss investment bank, lost £71 million in seconds while trying to sell 16 shares in Japanese advertising giant Dentsu at 600,000 yen each. He sold 610,000 shares at six yen each.

- May 2001: A trader at Lehman Brothers mistyped a trade and wiped £30 billion off the stock market. He wanted to sell £3 million of stock but typed too many zeros and sold £300 million. The bank suffered a £20,000 fine for his clumsiness.

- November 1999: A dealer put his elbow on the keyboard and inadvertently placed 600 trades in 16,000 of the Premier Oil's shares at 19p, worth more than £1.8 million.

STRATEGY 18

Be Wary of Overconfidence

"There are two kinds of people that lose money: those that know nothing and those that know everything. With two Nobel Prize winners in the house, Long-Term Capital Management fits the second case"

– R. Lenzner, *Forbes Magazine*, 1998

Is Overconfidence Good or Bad?

When you are lacking in confidence you are quite likely to be in an anxious or fearful state, and your actions and behaviour as a result are likely to keep you out of the markets. Although you won't be making much money, you certainly won't be losing too much either. But overconfidence will get you into the market more frequently and with bigger positions, and more so than might be your norm.

The results of trading in an overconfident manner can have a significant impact on your P&L – at best you will get big positive up swings, at worst you will get massive losses and drawdown.

Can you think of times when you have experienced overconfidence in your trading?

What was the result?

Exercise

Place a mark where you would place yourself on the following scales:

Worst driver on the road ◄———————————► *Best driver on the road*

Worst person at my job ◄———————————► *Best person at my job*

Least intelligent person I know ◄————————► *Most intelligent person I know*

Worst looking person I know ◄————————► *Best looking person I know*

Least likely to make it as a trader ◄————► *Most likely to make it as a trader*

The chances are that on most of the scales you have placed yourself at, or above, average. Is that true for you? Interestingly, research suggests that humans tend towards overconfidence. If, for example, the majority of traders fail or are unprofitable, then the fact that you are trading suggests that you are overconfident – you obviously did not expect to be in the large percentage that fail, did you?

People tend towards overconfidence

- 19% of people in the U.S. think they belong to the richest 1% of U.S. households.

- 82% of people say they are in the top 30% of safe drivers.

- 80% of students think they will finish in the top half of their class.

- 68% of lawyers in civil cases believe that their side will prevail.

- 81% of new business owners think their business has at least a 70% chance of success, but only 39% think any business like theirs would be likely to succeed.

- 86% of my old university class say they are better looking than their classmates.

(From *Behavioural Finance: Insights into Irrational Minds and Markets*, by James Montier)

Overconfidence or at least high confidence is needed for us to take on challenges, so it's useful in one form. However, as traders, what we need to be mindful of and aware of is the *fine distinction* between high confidence or conviction, and overconfidence.

"One of the key challenges that I think all traders have is in not getting overconfident. It is so easy to just increase your position sizing and take more risk when you are doing well."

– Tony Dicarlo, trader

Overcoming Overconfidence

So overconfidence may be natural – which leaves us with the question of *how* we overcome it in our trading?

The first step is to identify when traders are at risk of overconfidence and to then put in place specific actions to implement in those particular circumstances.

Reflect on your own trading. When are you most prone to overconfidence?

In my experience there are two key moments which tend to prompt strong levels of overconfidence in traders:

1. Following a win that is significantly greater than normal.

2. When the trader is on a winning run of trades or over a particular time period.

Understanding that these two particular situations can lead to overconfidence means that we should classify them as high risk. If trading is about managing risk, then trading is definitely about managing overconfidence. Now, if those two situations trigger overconfidence, then building some protocol around them may be very useful. The first element is awareness – knowing the situations and also the signs.

When you are getting overconfident, how do you know?

Signs that you are getting overconfident may include:

- Wanting to take bigger positions in the market.

- Trading more frequently than usual.

- Taking trades that are non-strategy trades and have little verifiable edge in the market.

- Not doing your trading preparation and/or evaluation.

- Generally putting less time and effort into your trading.

- Thoughts akin to making you the new market master; that this is easy, that you have cracked it, that you cannot lose or be beaten – all are warning signs, too!

If you notice yourself getting overconfident then what action can you take?

Overconfidence is a strong and powerful emotion; it is intense and fuelled and therefore carries momentum, so one of the fundamental strategies that you should consider employing is to break the momentum by stopping trading. Take a time-out and evaluate your trading, as well as your behaviours and actions. Then re-read/assess your trading strategy and look at how you will implement it going forward. If you really feel that you cannot stick to your trading strategy, then not trading until these feelings subside may be the best trade of all!

> **❝ Overconfidence is intense, and carries momentum, so it is critical to know how to break it. ❞**

Practical Strategy: Overcoming Overconfidence

Recognise the specific situations when you are prone to overconfidence and note these as being high-risk situations. When they occur, commit to taking preventative action.

Learn to recognise within yourself the thoughts, feelings and behaviours that occur as you move towards overconfidence. This can become like an early warning system that enables you to take action before it is too late. This requires and develops a high level of self-awareness – a strong feature of successful traders.

Devise specific strategies to implement once you recognise that overconfidence is occurring or is a strong possibility. This might include taking time out from the markets, being restrictive on trades being taken, and monitoring carefully your position sizing.

Real Life Example

"Most people make the mistake of increasing their bets as soon as they start making money. That is a quick way to get wiped out."

– Marty Schwartz, in *Market Wizards*

A classic example of overconfidence in traders is graduates who have just come off the training programme and onto the trading floor. For weeks they have been conditioned and guided in managing risk, being selective, and trading their particular strategy, as well as schooled in following a large number of rituals to support their trading – including preparation and evaluation.

But over the years I have seen, time and time again, traders such as these with less than three months live trading experience suddenly have a good one or two days trading or put together a string of good trading results – and then suddenly start increasing the size of their positions, running trades through their stops, losing focus on their risk and money management strategies and taking trades that are higher in risk, and which they have been warned off trading.

In fact, even as I am writing this, I am involved in email correspondence regarding a number of recent trainees that have taken high-risk trading positions into the front month of oil contracts on the day of delivery! This is ludicrous behaviour for a trainee trader. Following some good P&L days, mainly achieved by higher risk trading strategies (driven by the desire to make money quickly rather than progress slowly), the traders are now taking even greater risk to try and increase their results.

They are, in essence, dopamine victims. Dopamine, the pleasure chemical, is released in our bodies when we have a positive experience; however, to get a release again from a similar situation, the next experience has to be even more pleasurable or exciting. In traders, this leads to them taking more and more risk – as only by doing so will they get the dopamine kick!

STRATEGY 19

Deal With Negative Emotions Positively

"I want to know if the people that I am going to work with can handle the stress, pressures and high demands of trading in a positive way. This is really important to me."

– Lex Van Dam, hedge fund manager

Recognising Performance Limiting Emotions

What states would you say are negative for you? Which feelings detract from your trading performance? What emotions do you experience as a trader that prevent you from performing to the best of your abilities? How do they do this?

How often do you experience these emotions?

How do you deal with them?

Emotions are natural and a part of being human. It is critical in my opinion to recognise that learning to identify and understand your emotions is more important, in most cases, than trying to suppress or control them. One of the most useful areas to develop awareness in is in assessing which of the emotions you experience are performance-enhancing; i.e. those which are Ideal Trading States, as against those which are performance-limiting.

When we look at classifying emotions as *positive* or *limiting* we have to do this in the context of the environment we are in; and so in our case we are looking at this purely from a trading perspective.

States that might be perceived as being limiting for traders include:

- Anger
- Frustration
- Fear
- Anxiety
- Boredom
- Greed
- Hope
- Stress
- Overconfidence

How Negative States Affect Performance

Negative states have an adverse effect on performance because the emotions that you are accessing do not enable you to perform the actions that are required for trading effectively. When we experience high intensity negative states such as anger, fear, frustration and any states that create stress within us, we experience changes in our body chemistry that affect our ability to perform.

Under these conditions, the blood flow to the cortex (rational part of the brain required for logical thinking, objective decision making) is restricted, resulting in cortical inhibition, a process of shutting down of the 'smart brain' – leaving us with access only to our emotional centres. The result of this is that we are now trading our emotions and not our strategy. When we are in such states our ability to trade our plan, run profits, cut losses and operate any other logical trading process is dramatically reduced and the risk of poor quality, undisciplined trading is increased.

So it is vital, then, to be able to recognise when your state has shifted to a limiting state. How do you do this?

Think of a time when you were experiencing a limiting state. How did you know you had that state? What were the signs? What were you thinking? What were you imagining? What was your physiology – breathing/muscle tension – like? How about your body language?

The aim is to recognise the *signatures* of your emotions at such times, in order to be able to spot the early signs that you are shifting into a negative state or are in one. You can then act upon this as appropriate.

Dealing With Negative States Positively

Awareness is the first stage of dealing with your negative emotions. This can be done through 'checking in' (see STRATEGY 11). Ask yourself, "How/what am I feeling? How do I know?" The second stage is to deal with the feeling.

Practical Strategy: Dealing With Negative States Positively

Emotions as Messengers

Think of emotions as messengers.

Ask, "What is the message behind this emotion?"

And in doing so you are taking away from purely focussing on what you are feeling, to why you are feeling. Once you have identified the emotion and the reason why you are feeling it, then you are ready to take action on the feedback you have received.

Go Into Neutral

When you are in a negatively-charged state it can be extremely difficult to switch from that state straight into a positive one. To help you to transition from a negative state into a more positive state, it can be very useful to go into a neutral state first. Try this very simple exercise to achieve a neutral state, and then when you have achieved this, and feel ready, you can then use the Ideal Trading State strategies (STRATEGY 11) to move into positive territory.

First – focus on your heart. You may find it easier to do this by placing a hand on your heart, or by looking towards your heart area, or even by listening to your heartbeat.

Secondly – breathe in to a count of five and out to a count of five. This rhythm has been proven by cardiac research at the HeartMath Institute in the USA to be very powerful in achieving positive physiological effects. It may feel uncomfortable at first, so perseverance and practice are key.

Keep focussed on the heart and perform the breathing for as long as you need to, until you can feel that you are calmer and ready to shift to a more positive state.

STRATEGY 20

Embrace Risk and Uncertainty

"The core of a trader's role is making decisions under conditions of uncertainty and risk. It is widely recognised that trading is a difficult job that places enormous pressures on individuals – in terms of the complexity and the flow of information, the major consequences that can flow from decisions, and the limited time frame and resources they have to make decisions."

– 'Traders, Risks, Decisions and Management' in *Financial Markets*, Fenton-O'Creevy, Nicholson, Soane and Willman

A Challenging Cocktail

As traders we are making our money from trading the markets, from making financial decisions in an environment of risk and uncertainty. If there was a formula to describe what goes on in challenging decisions, it might look something like this:

Risk + Uncertainty + Money = Challenging Decisions

If you then add into that short time frames, and the pressure and stress that can be generated due to the possible consequences of those decisions, it is not difficult to see why trading is so difficult, and so few people are able to excel at it.

To become a trader you need to embrace risk and uncertainty, as they are an integral part of the trading world. You need to develop approaches to help you to accept and manage your risk in a way that still enables you to make profits, and you need to learn to cope with the uncertainty that trading brings.

Embracing Risk

"Psychologically, most of us prefer comfort and safety to risk-taking."

– Ari Kiev, *The Psychology of Risk*

Do you consider yourself a risk-taker? Do you accept that a trade has a non-guaranteed, probable outcome? Do you believe you are taking a risk when you put on a trade? Have you accepted the possible consequences?

If you are going to embrace risk then your answers to those questions all need to be a resounding "YES!" To be a successful trader you need to embrace risk, and this means that any trade that you enter, no matter how much you may want it to be a winner, or how confident you are, still has a non-guaranteed, probable outcome.

Even if you have an established trading strategy with a 70% win ratio, you are still going to lose statistically on three out of every ten trades – although, because we do not know the distribution of the outcomes of our trading, it could easily be a lot more than this in any given small sample.

So every trade you place has a risk. It is easy, especially when trading is going well, to focus on reward – however, a key part of sustained trading must be risk management. When you place a trade, if you accept that there is risk, then you should also accept that there is the chance of this trade being a loser. Only when you totally accept that you are taking a risk, that your outcome is non-guaranteed, and that the outcome could be a loss, can you experience trading in a more positive and free state of mind, reducing fear, hesitation and stress and enabling you to achieve your trading potential. Without this, simple anxiety unnecessarily gnaws away.

Practical Strategy: Embracing Risk

Develop a Risk Mindset

Embracing risk is really all about developing a mindset, a collection of beliefs that are empowering and useful to you as regards risk and trading, and these might include:

- I accept that as a trader I am taking risk/I am a risk-taker

- I accept that every trade has a non-guaranteed, probable outcome

- I accept that I can lose on any given trade

- I am a trader. I am trading based on the principles of risk and reward. I have to be willing to take risk to capture my potential rewards

Identify Your Risk Comfort Zone

It is also important to be aware of your own attitude towards risk taking in terms of how risk averse or not you are. This is of particular value to you when you are developing your trading strategy. If your trading risk profile and your personal risk profile are not aligned, then there is the potential for conflict.

Take a Risk Inventory

Make a list of all the possible risks that are possible within your trading and then write down next to each one how you will deal with that risk. This can help you to plan for and manage your risk.

"Only trade with the amount of risk that you're comfortable with. Positions that are excessively large can affect your perception and decision making, which makes you far more likely to make mistakes."

– R. R., trader

Embracing Uncertainty

Uncertainty is not easy to deal with. From one perspective it would be great if, in life, we knew what was going to happen all of the time; but, on the other hand, it might actually take out some of the challenge, joy and rewards. Many people who are in trading say that they like the fact that no one day is the same as another, that they

> **“** Trading is engaging because it is unpredictable; so uncertainty is fundamental, and not inevitably bad. It just needs to be adapted to. **”**

would not enjoy being in a job that was predictable – in choosing trading for this reason you also have to accept that what makes trading different every day is the uncertainty! Trading the markets is full of uncertainty. The market conditions can change from day to day, and trading strategies that have worked so well for so long can suddenly appear to stop working.

To embrace uncertainty means to accept that there is uncertainty; to understand that you will never totally understand what is going to happen next, and in fact that you do not need to.

Traders get frustrated when market conditions change and this yields lower than expected P&L returns. However, this is a part of trading. The expert trader accepts this and is always watching and monitoring the markets and how they are trading; and through their evaluation processes they are able to identify specific changes in behaviour, and adjust their trading approach accordingly – whether it be by reducing risk, not trading, or adopting a new trading strategy.

Practical Strategy: Embracing Uncertainty

Accept that uncertainty is a part of trading. If you cannot accept this, then trading may not be for you.

Make Every Market Condition Your Favourite

Gary Player, the golfer, was once playing a big tournament on a particular course. Rumour has it that, when he arrived, the green-keeper, with whom he was very good friends, said to him,

"Gary, be careful. With all the hot weather we have been having, the greens are really running fast."

"Thanks," replied Gary. "I love it when the greens play fast."

Later in the year, playing at the same course, Player arrived and was greeted by the green-keeper again. This time he warned him to be careful, as the weather had been horrid and the course was carrying a lot of water; the greens were playing slow.

"Thanks," replied Gary. "I love it when the greens play slow."

One way of dealing with uncertainty is to build positive attitudes towards the different market conditions that might arise, and the different challenges that trading in them brings. Love to trade the markets when they are quiet, and love to trade the markets when they are busy and volatile.

STRATEGY 21

Pull the Trigger – Overcome Hesitation and Fear

"Decision-making – either get someone to teach you what to do, or spend a very long time figuring it out for yourself! Once you've done that, trust your gut and your right hand. Ignore the voice in your head. PRESS THE BUTTON!"

– Matt Blom, trader

Is Interference Blocking Your Performance?

Have you ever seen a trade set-up from your strategy and *not* taken it? What stopped you? Not pulling the trigger can be extremely frustrating for a trader, especially when you only seem to remember every time that you didn't execute and then the markets went *right* towards where you would have made profit!

When you don't do something that you wanted to do, there must have been a reason why – something that held you back, some interference with your normal strategy. In his book *The Inner Game Of Tennis*, Tim Gallwey identifies the formula:

$$Pe = Po - I$$

(In other words, Performance = Potential – Interference)

A person will perform to their potential, minus any interference that occurs. In terms of not pulling the trigger, what we essentially want to be able to do is *identify* what the interference is that is stopping you from executing.

Below is a list of reasons, or possible causes of interference, that may stop traders from pulling the trigger. I have then presented a number of potential solutions that may help.

Identifying the Interference

1. No belief that you have a strategy with an edge or positive expectancy in the market

If you are in this situation, then your interference is possibly derived from self-doubt and a lack of confidence. This is natural, since having a strategy is a key step forward in executing more consistently; and without one that you have confidence in, you must either fail from genuine problems that do exist in it, or from simple lack of nerve. Testing and feedback is the answer! And once you have tested and gained feedback from your trading, and have done your homework, you will over time gain more and more confidence in your system – and rightly so.

2. Fear of loss

Traders who are afraid of losing will often enough actually create interference that prevents them from pulling the trigger. Fear as an emotion enables us to withdraw – in the case of trading, to not trade; to withdraw from the markets.

How are you creating your fear of loss?

Is it from taking excessive risk and aiming to trade positions that are above your threshold and propensity for loss? From a self-protection perspective, by not trading you are saving yourself from the pain of loss. If you reduce your trading size and take less risk, you may find that your ability to actually execute improves dramatically. In fact, I would say in the majority of cases I have come across where traders are having challenges pulling the trigger, excessive risk-taking is one of the core causes. Consider your sizing in relation to your own threshold for loss, your trading account, and, where appropriate, your personal wealth.

I remember delivering a seminar on improving trading strategy execution and one of the key points was trading appropriate size and managing risk so that you are free to execute. One of the people who attended that seminar emailed me a few days later to say how, after months of getting frustrated and annoyed about not pulling the trigger on their trades, they had made a significant breakthrough with their trade execution.

What had changed?

They had reduced their trading size to the minimum – reduced the level of stress and fear that had been keeping them out of the market – and were now free to execute without hesitation.

You could also be afraid of loss simply by dint of hating to lose, regardless of the amount. This shows that, as a trader, you have not embraced one of the fundamental facts of trading life; that losses are a natural part of the trading cycle. No one likes to lose, but unless you deeply and truly accept its statistical inevitability then there will always be interference in your trading, and you will not achieve your full trading potential.

3. Anxiety

Some people are by nature quite anxious and tend to worry a lot about things. Trading, and particularly short time frame trading, presents lots of opportunities for anxiety to occur. There is great uncertainty in trading; every trade has a non-guaranteed outcome – and both of these factors can compound or prompt feelings of anxiety. People who have consistently high levels of anxiety may have to decide that, perhaps, trading is not for them – or find a way to trade that reduces their anxiety levels to the minimum possible.

4. Lack of strategy

If you have no trading strategy, then, by default, you have no identifiable trading opportunities. How do you know when to trade? You don't! Every price movement is a possible trade, but you are never sure whether to take it or not. Defining your strategy and the trading opportunities that it presents is a fundamental step for you to take with your trading.

5. Past experience

Sometimes a past experience in the market can leave you both scarred and scared! I have found that bigger losses than normally experienced, or a string of losses and a period of drawdown that is much greater than the norm, can all impact on a trader's ability to pull the trigger. At a core level they are experiencing a lack of confidence and trust in their system or themselves. As they try to execute, thoughts and images of the past pop into their head and generate feelings and interference that ends in hesitation or no action at all.

Practical Strategy: Overcoming Past Negative Experiences

Imagine sitting in a cinema. See the screen in front of you. On the screen, replay the negative event that occurred.

Now ask yourself what you can learn from that event, and make a note of this; commit to acting on the information you deduce.

Now, on the screen, replay the event again, but this time make any images you see fade in colour, become more blurred and less clear, turn down any sounds that you can hear and now make the screen smaller, and smaller and smaller; and send it further and further away, until it fades into a dot in the distance.

Reassess your feelings about the event. If they are still strong, then repeat the final step above over and over again, until the feelings are reduced.

This technique works because it helps in some senses to change your subjective experience of the event. By changing the structure of your thinking about the event, you change, in a way, your experience of the event.

6. Trading not to lose

Sometimes I have come across or worked with traders who tell me that they are having problems executing their trades, only for it to transpire, through our conversations, that they are focussed not on trading, but on trading not to lose. And they are actually achieving their goal, because the easiest way to not lose money trading is... to not trade!

The choice, however, is not between trading *not* to lose, and trading simply to win; between impairing conservatism and reckless daring. As high-performance traders, we are trading to win, to make money, *whilst managing risk* – in fact we are managing risk as a primary concern, and looking at making profits, in some ways, secondarily.

7. Fear of being wrong

Some traders do not like to be wrong; in fact, from an ego perspective, none of us really like to be wrong. If you interpret a losing trade as being wrong, then you are going to naturally not want to incur any losing trades; and again, this can best be achieved by not trading, or by being very cautious and hesitant. But it is, itself, in error; and merely deals out loss pre-emptively, by denying you prudent, profitable trades.

8. Perfectionism

Traders who are perfectionists often have challenges in executing trades. They are waiting for the 'perfect' set-up to execute from. This rarely exists, as there is always that extra indicator or piece of confirmation that they could really do with. Trading, like golf, is not a game of perfection. It can be a game of precision and excellence when performed well; but trades, like golf shots, can more often than not be reviewed and agonised over, with a retrospective idealism never once practical in the moment of execution.

It is important to realise that perfectionism, though arising from positive intentions, rarely brings out the full potential in a trader.

You have to learn to be happy to go at 90%-95% and sometimes less – if you wait for all the lights to go on, you will rarely trade, and will ultimately end up frustrated.

9. Changes in market conditions

When market conditions change, as they do, both on a short-term and longer-term basis, it has an impact on the results produced by a trader's strategy. These can obviously sometimes be unfavourable, as the match between the strategy and the market conditions is out of sync, and the trader incurs losses and drawdown outside of the norm.

If the trader cannot specifically identify what has changed, and adapt his trading strategy appropriately, then he is left in a situation where the level of uncertainty experienced is increased and this leads to lower levels of confidence. In this situation it is critical to analyse the markets and to assess what is happening; and where you can identify ways in which to alter your trading strategy, do so. Where the time frame of the change is short or you are unable to really identify what is happening within the markets, then you may want to consider lowering your risk exposure. I like to explain this by using three variables – uncertainty, confidence and risk.

Where uncertainty is high, confidence is likely to be lowered, and as a result it makes sense to reduce your risk exposure until your confidence levels improve. Where uncertainty is high, confidence is low and risk is high, the trader is setting themselves up for some potentially large losses and drawdown.

Real Life Example: Helping a Trader to Improve Their Execution

Tim was a novice fixed income futures trader who had been trading the live markets for three months, following his graduate trading programme. He came for coaching, concerned that he was seeing trading opportunities but not taking them.

To help him, we agreed on the following actions:

1. Reduce trading size to minimise any worry of loss/being wrong.

2. Focus his daily trading objectives on trading to make money: seeing opportunities and taking them, based on a written goal; supporting this with affirmation and visualisation.

3. Mentally conditioning the process by reaffirming when he did execute; and by mentally replaying times when he did not execute, as though, this time, he had.

4. Evaluating and measuring his progress.

Within seven days his execution rate (percentage of trades taken from those that he had seen) increased from 30%, the benchmark, to 42%, and then up to 50%. Once he got to this point he had greater confidence in his abilities and in his strategy, and he was able to go on to achieve levels of over 60% and make a solid improvement to his trading account.

STRATEGY 22

Understand That More is Not Always More – Avoid Overtrading

"Do not confuse activity with achievement."

– John Wooden, legendary NCAA basketball coach

Overtrading is Not Cheap

Overtrading can be a common problem, particularly for day traders. There is a real financial cost to overtrading, in terms of commissions/spread being paid. There is also the fact that many of these trades may not form a genuine part of one's trading strategy, and therefore will possess less edge, lower expectancy, and a consequent greater propensity towards loss.

One of the first things to be aware of is *when* you are overtrading. To do this you will need to have some kind of baseline measure to work from, and by which you can assess your activity by noting its variance from this value. Of course, there may be situations when this is to be accepted; for example, when the markets are particularly busy, and because of this provide more trading opportunities than the norm.

Why Do Traders Overtrade?

Gambling and excitement

The trader is trading the markets for excitement and for fun, rather than for profit; much the same as most people who play in the casino.

Solution

If your goal is purely to have fun and to create excitement, then you need to accept the fact that profitability is unlikely. If you want profitability from your trading then you need to make a shift in your motives and goals away from fun and excitement towards a more professional and structured approach, with trading profitably as your desired outcome.

No strategy

The trader has no defined strategy and therefore there are no parameters to determine when to trade or not. Hence, any given price movement or market move provides the temptation to trade.

Traders in this situation are very prone to chasing the markets and often find that, as they go long, the market comes off, and as they go short, the market rallies! It feels as if the market is out to get them. Does that sound familiar?

Solution

The most important area that you can focus on is to develop a trading strategy with an edge and a positive expectancy!

Boredom

In quiet market conditions, when the trader is spending large amounts of time at the screen, there will be periods when there are little or no trading opportunities. This is a natural part of trading! This is the stakeout scenario that the police and special forces encounter.

However, these situations present the trader with the challenge of being patient and staying out of the market. For some traders this is very difficult – particularly those who are new to trading, those who are trading for excitement, those who are over enthusiastic or those who need to make money!

Solution

If you are overly enthusiastic and perhaps new to trading, then you need to balance your enthusiasm of wanting to trade anything that moves with the need to develop your discipline to follow your trading strategy. Patience is a great skill to gain as a trader, so do not see not such fallow periods as time wasted, but rather as time well spent in cultivating this skill. Anyone can place a trade; keeping out of the market and not trading is far more difficult.

For the others, a really important question to ask yourself is, "Am I trading to relieve boredom or to make money?"

You need to make money; you are in a desperate situation

This is one of the worst emotions or positions to trade in. It is a strong and powerful state but also not conducive to good trading, as your whole decision making focus is on making money and not on trading your strategy, and the two are not always the same. If your strategy is designed, of course, to make profits – what are you doing abandoning it, in the hope of... making profits!

Solution

Assessing your financial needs and your trading performance is very important. Anything that you can do to relieve the necessity to make money will be a great step forward for you.

Enthusiasm

New traders are blessed with enthusiasm! Traders who are entering new markets, or using new trading methodologies, are also prone to over enthusiasm and a too-great willingness to get involved. Whilst this enthusiasm is undoubtedly positive to a certain extent, there is also the dark side to consider – being over enthusiastic and looking, recklessly, for *any* opportunity to trade.

Solution

Maintain your enthusiasm but re-direct it towards developing your ability to trade your strategy when trades appear, as well as developing the discipline required to stick to your strategy. If you have to trade, consider doing it on the simulator/demo account where the costs are considerably lower! Also consider using your enthusiasm to do any reading or development work that may be required or any other trading-specific tasks.

Lack of patience

Traders who lack patience will over-trade, taking opportunities that are not a part of their trading strategy.

Solution

Tom Hougaard describes the need for patience like this:

> Be patient. I run a live trading room. The hardest part is to make subscribers
> understand that a professional day trader does not trade every 5 minutes.
> Sitting in silence, waiting for an opportunity is much like a cheetah, hunting
> for food. Not every chase results in a kill, and if the cheetah runs after every
> opportunity, it will soon run out of energy. Traders are similar in nature.
>
> (www.tradertom.com)

 Trader Top Tips

"Once, I turned up pre-open, logged on, sat in front of my screen, watched
every tick for the whole day, thought about what I would do, waited for the
close – and went home. Without ever entering an order. Just to prove to myself
I could. After that day, I rarely, if ever, over-traded, or traded when I shouldn't
have. I knew I needed to be able to not get involved and to be patient; doing
this exercise worked for me."

– Matt Blom, trader

The hunting analogy is a useful one and is shared by Van Tharp who calls the
waiting and monitoring part of the trading cycle 'stalking'. This metaphor can
be useful to embrace as a trader. I also liken it to police officers or special forces
soldiers in a stake-out or observation post – lots of patience and waiting, for a
few moments of execution. Understanding that actually being in a position is
only one part of the trading cycle is key. Recognise that execution –
enter/manage/exit – is only three-fifths of the trading cycle and that
monitoring and spotting are the other three-fifths. And, further, that it is likely
that you will spend a large amount of your time in the monitor and spot
portions, as opposed to the enter/manage and exit stages.

Expectations – you need to develop realistic expectations about what you want
from the market and understand that the market will determine how many

trading opportunities there are whilst you can control how many you see and how well you trade them.

Spend a trading session just watching the market, resisting the urge to trade, or give yourself a target of reducing the number of trades you make in a given period by half to make yourself more selective and patient.

In revenge!

Where traders have lost money through a trading loss, a mistake, fat finger, or what have you, there is often an urge to 'get my money back'. Whilst the intention behind such a thought is positive, the ensuing behaviour is often not. Traders who chase losses will be skewed towards taking any potential trade that could make money, regardless of whether it is a strategy trade or not; the mental framework, the goal as such, is now to make money and not to make money by trading the strategy flawlessly. The anchor is up, and there is no telling where you may get blown.

Solution

Where you have had a big loss, or lost a large amount of money through a series of trades, you may wish to incorporate a ritual of taking a tim-eout. This time-out allows you time to readdress your trading state and to refocus, but also, and importantly, breaks the behavioural pattern of *lose money-feel angry-get money back*.

The time-out interrupts the pattern and enables you to refocus and run a different mental programme – perhaps using the coherence technique at these times, as it helps to get you back to a neutral and more positive state, with the ability to make more logical and rational decisions. But something more natural, or whatever works for you, following the time-out, is recommended too.

Costs of Overtrading

There are real costs to overtrading in terms of:

- The extra commission charges and/or spreads paid.
- The emotional frustration of knowing that you are overtrading.

- The longer-term damage incurred through taking trades that are not a part of your trading strategy, thereby ingraining and practising the act of being ill-disciplined.

These costs have a short and longer-term impact on your trading performance and profitability. Overtrading should be carefully monitored. Take a trader-as-risk behavioural risk management approach and be aware of the particular circumstances when you are more prone to overtrading. Monitor these situations carefully as they arise, and act accordingly – dependent on what is driving your behaviour.

Practical Strategy: Reducing Overtrading

Reflect on your trading – use your logs and journals – and identify the key times/situations when you are prone to overtrading.

Review the common causes of overtrading and their solutions in this chapter and apply any that are appropriate as preventative measures.

Make a note of where your risk of overtrading is highest, and most likely to occur. For each of these situations, decide how you will monitor if you start to overtrade, and also what you will do once you have recognised it. It may be as simple as stopping trading, and taking some time out to slow down and reflect on what has happened.

STRATEGY 23

Transform Adversity Into Challenge

"Of all the virtues we can learn, no trait is more essential for survival and more likely to improve the quality of life than the ability to transform adversity into an enjoyable challenge."

– Mihaly Csikszentmihalyi

Failure and Adversity Enable Success

All traders go through tough times at some points in their trading career. It is a natural part of the path to success: challenges have to be endured and survived in order to take you to the next level.

I remember once reading about New Zealand triathlete Hamish Carter, who was really focussed and determined to win the Olympics in Sydney in 2000. He was a very talented athlete, trained hard, and dedicated his whole life to the achievement of that goal. Imagine, then, his disappointment at finishing 26th.

Following that setback he decided to re-evaluate his whole training process, lifestyle, psychology – everything. He then set about another four-year training cycle, working towards the 2004 games in Athens. At those games he finished first! He achieved his goal, his dream. And he categorically stated that it had taken that loss in 2000 to give him

> " Challenges have to be endured and survived in order to take you to the next level. "

the drive to really make some changes in his approach; that it was that loss that had given him the mental toughness to be able to win in 2004. In his own words:

"The key to success is failure. If I didn't have Sydney to wallow in, I wouldn't have won in Athens. It [Sydney] was the worst day of my life, but one of the most important."

When you read *Market Wizards* you will find countless examples of traders who lost all of their money, sometimes several times, before making the changes required to allow them to move to the next level.

Tough times make people tough. Getting through these times is often a function of desire and passion to achieve the end goal, as well as self-belief and the mental and physical resilience to keep going and endure this period.

When Things Don't Seem to Work – Be Proactive!

"I have had many ups and downs in trading, but I truly can say that it is the hard times when you learn the most about yourself. I feel that when things are going well you tend to become slightly less focussed on the reasons why you're being successful. It is only when you go through the hard times that you really become introspective and this is when you discover what makes you a successful trader and what allows you to go forward and get through the difficulties."

– Lawrie Inman, trader

Sometimes in trading it can feel like nothing is working, that the markets are against you and that you are destined to lose money. I am sure that many of you have experienced that feeling, right? And it is perfectly natural... but what do you do when you are in that situation?

It is easy to get into a downward spiral, getting more and more negative, which in turn makes peak trading more difficult. And then the results *still* don't come – and so it continues, on and on into the land of doom and gloom! This continues until maybe something happens in the market, and you make some money; an act, perhaps, of randomness occurs, you profit and your mood is lifted and promotes your rise back upwards. The question is, though, how long do you wait for that random market event to provide some profit and the psychological pick-up? In this situation you are like a sailing boat on the ocean with no rudder, at the mercy of the wind and waves; in fact you are in a psychological state of *helplessness* which has been much studied by the prominent American psychologist Martin Seligman.

Have you ever had a car that broke down? If so, what was your attitude and approach? Did you view it as though the whole car was broken, and did you wait for some random event to occur and for the car to start working again? Probably not! You may have tried to identify where the problem was specifically, i.e. it was not the whole car that was broken but rather a part of the car, and this may have been done by yourself or with the help of a professional in the automotive industry. You then probably decided to get the car fixed and then got back driving. The key thing is that you were active in getting the problem resolved, that you looked to identify where the specific challenge was and were then able to resolve the issue and move forward.

It is no different with trading. You are not at the mercy of luck and chaos.

When you are having a tough time in your trading it is not the whole market or the whole of *you* that is suddenly not working! You need to take a proactive approach to resolving the challenge that you are facing, and aim to identify the specific areas in which your performance is being affected. For example, perhaps your trade entries are not as good as they have been previously, maybe through being a little impatient or a little hesitant, or perhaps some of the indicators that you have been using previously are not working as well within a changing set of market conditions. Maybe your trade exits are not as good as they have been, perhaps your stops or profit targets need to be adjusted; maybe there are elements of your strategy that need to be adjusted to get a better match to the current market conditions; perhaps you are tired, or challenges outside of trading have been affecting your trading. Whatever it may be, aim to identify the specific challenge and then be proactive in resolving it.

> "If you want to see a great fighter at his best then watch him when he is getting beat."
>
> – Sugar Ray Robinson

Consider what your reaction has been when faced with such situations in your trading. Do you suffer from helplessness, and wait for random events to bail you out, or are you proactive and focussed on solving the problem? Traders who take a more dynamic problem-focussed approach to their trading challenges are more likely to return to higher levels of trading more quickly, and will most likely have greater levels of resilience and feel more in control of their trading outcomes.

Where Are You Focussed?

In 2004 I was asked to go and work with a group of traders in Chicago who were having a tough time, and I noticed through my discussions with them that they were doing two things in particular:

- Becoming very P&L focussed

- Focussing on what was going wrong or not working

In the coaching and training that I did with them I taught them a variety of strategies and techniques for coping with such times; but the core and fundamental strategy that I got them to utilise was what I call the 'triangle of strength'. This involves focussing your trading around three dimensions.

1. Positives

What is going well?

It is so easy, when you are having a tough time, to become overly focussed on what is not working. And if, in some respects, we get what we focus on, then this leads to you just getting more of what you are already getting – and don't want! A shift in focus to looking for what is *going well*, and what *is* working, is not easy. But it is doable; and it is a skill that needs to be developed as a part of tough thinking.

2. Strengths

What are your strengths and how can you best utilise them to help you in this situation?

When times are tough you can either give up or you can get your head down and work your way out of it. When traders take the second option they can actually go too far, and start to get so immersed in their situation that they are not being objective or strategic about *what* they are doing and *how* they are doing it.

They just keep working harder and harder, hoping that their hard work will be rewarded. But all traders have particular *strengths*, and these ought especially to be called on times of difficulty or weakness. They could be strengths in the areas of knowledge, execution skills, trading ability, resilience, motivation and persistence, staying focussed, work ethic, composure, strategy development – what have you. These are critical resources.

When times are tough it is useful to assess your strengths (see STRATEGY 8) and see how you can utilise them most effectively in this situation; not unlike if you were managing a team, and the team was having a tough time, you might look at the strengths of particular members of the team and redeploy them accordingly, to make up for weakness and to bolster performance.

3. Controllables

In difficult times, when the pressure is on, it can become easy to focus too much on factors that are outside of your control, particularly, in trading terms, the market. Blaming and complaining about market conditions does nothing to improve your performance – it might only help in the short-term in you having a quick moan and feeling better! Performance is always enhanced when focus is on a well-designed process and the process is controllable. This is no different when times are tough. You need to create your processes, identify what is controllable and then focus on those aspects of your performance.

Practical Strategy: Getting Out of Performance Slumps

The meaning of any event is, in some respects, the meaning that you give it. If you have a tough time and you start to say that you are in a 'slump', what does that mean to you? If being in a slump means being in the long-term midst of a negative and undesirable set of trading events, then that may not be the most optimistic or helpful label! Although I have used the word slump within this chapter, I actively encourage traders not to use that word as it often has negative connotations, and can keep a trader trapped inside their experience as they repeatedly reinforce that they are in a slump. Be wary of your language and aim to frame the situation as positively as possible – "I am having a bit of a challenge," or, "Things are not quite going to plan", etc, etc.

See any bad patches as temporary. A part of being resilient, as discussed, is having an optimistic explanatory style, and in this case the key aspect here is keeping the permanence factor short, i.e. seeing any situation that you are in as being short-term and temporary. If you expect your slump to go on for months then, guess what, it might just do so!

Take a step back and actively analyse what has happened. If the results that you are getting have dramatically changed, then something must have altered. The two core components that make up your trading P&L are the markets and you. So where there has been a drop off in results away from the norm I would assess, firstly, the market conditions; and then, secondly, whether you have initiated any changes in your style of trading, and beyond that whether there have been any changes outside of trading, e.g. life events.

Use the Strengths, Positives and Controllables triangle. List your strengths and how you can utilise them most effectively. List the controllables and areas for you to focus your attention on. Each day list at least one – and preferably more – positives.

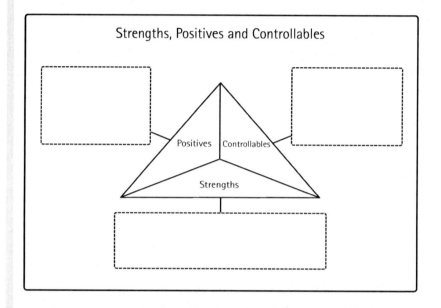

Monitor your emotional state – check in regularly, if you think it advisable – do everything you can to maintain as high a level of state as you can, as this we know has such a big impact on your performance capability. Being depressed and fed-up is not an ideal trading state, and the chances of you returning to form are minimal, unless you are saved by market events. Be aware of your physiology and body language, and also monitor the quality of your self-talk. If you are using self-talk that is negative and limiting, then get into the habit of catching yourself. Say "STOP", and then replace what you said with something more positive and useful.

It is particularly important during such times to pay attention to your health and well-being, to make sure that you are getting good quality sleep, that you are eating well and drinking plenty of water, exercising (the best way to burn off stress!) and getting some downtime to recover. When times are tough, energy expenditure is high; and so you need to focus on making deposits into your energy bank with such good habits.

Start each day and trading session by recalling times in the past when you have traded well and achieved positive results. It is essential to keep the 'success circuits' in the brain lit and activated, in order to be able to replicate this level of performance in the future. If you are not getting the results that you want in your trading in reality, and you spend significant amounts of time replaying this in your mind, then you are simply, I would argue, programming yourself for more of the same.

Take an ideal trader perspective. *What would the ideal trader do in this situation?* This can help you to adjust your level of thinking and to take a different view of events – as Einstein is said to have remarked, "You cannot solve a problem with the same thinking by which it was created." So to get out of the problem, you need to take a different level of thinking. This technique can actually work remarkably well!

STRATEGY 24

When Times Are Great, Keep Them Great

"The biggest hurdle seems to be successfully MAKING money. It breeds laziness, over-confidence, and in some cases arrogance. And any one of those will lead to making less or giving it back."

– Matt Blom

W e all know that when trading results are not where you want them to be, trading is pretty tough. Having the resilience to get through these times is critical. This can be a testing time, and can have an impact on the ability to sustain high performance in attitude and behaviour.

However, something really interesting that I have noticed with traders is that actually one of the most dangerous times in terms of a threat to sustaining high performance is when things are going well; and the better they are going, the greater the threat. I have seen many traders work hard to achieve high performance and success in trading, only to fall off the wagon (so to speak). Why is this?

> "It's far too easy to become complacent and to 'coast'; committing yourself to continued improvement requires discipline and focus, without discipline you will probably fall by the wayside."

> – Stewart Hampton

As the traders above point out so clearly, the two key challenges here are overconfidence and complacency. It is easy and natural to back off slightly when things are going well, and the longer the period goes on for, the easier and more likely it becomes. This is a high-risk time – when we consider the concept of trader-as-risk, this would be on my list of conditions to flag up.

What Can Be Done?

The most important factor in this situation is developing self-awareness that you are actually moving into a time of higher risk, as your behaviour may change – this is trader-as-risk monitoring. You are the greatest risk in your trading, and if your behaviour changes then discipline, performance and P&L may all also be affected. Being aware that you are having a good run and then being aware of any signs that your attitudes or behaviours are changing is important.

In my work with proprietary trading groups this is something that we would be monitoring for in the traders' metrics. Where performance moves greatly above the trader's moving average (we have been using three-month as our standard one) for P&L and stays above that, we would be monitoring that trader and making sure that they were staying focussed and disciplined, sticking to their strategy and maintaining their work ethic. We are looking for changes in attitude and behaviour, as these will precede or trigger changes in performance and ultimately P&L. This is something that I would strongly encourage any trader to do, and is why trade logs and journals are such important assets.

During these periods, it tends to be a warning flag when you stop doing your pre-trade preparation or you are not doing it as well as you could be, when you stop doing your evaluations or again do them but with little real thought or effort, and when you start considering taking extra risk either in terms of your position sizing or the trades you are taking.

Practical Strategy: Staying Focussed When Trading is Going Well

Awareness of performance

Be aware that you are on a good run; perhaps through looking at how your current performance is against historical performance (using moving averages can be very useful here).

Awareness of behaviour and mindset

Monitor your trading behaviours and your mindset:

- Have you ceased or reduced the quality of any of your key trading tasks? (Make a list of those you have routinely undertaken in times of past high performance. See if you can stick to this, or what falls away, and how badly.)

- Are you deviating from you trading strategy?

- Do you want to take excessive risks?

- Have you become less focussed on your trading generally?

- Are you spending more or less time trading than you do on average?

- Have you noticed any changes in your thoughts about trading? (e.g. "This is easy"; "I have cracked it"; "I just can't lose", etc)

Control

Make a list of key tasks to complete each time you trade, and key aspects of trading to focus on. Keep a record of whether you actually followed through on these each day. If you are consistently following all of your trading processes, then great. If not, take it as a warning light. Stop trading, and re-evaluate.

Part Three

Evaluation, Analysis and Improving and
Sustaining Performance

STRATEGY 25

Learn More – Keep Getting Better

"He who stops being better, stops being good."

– Oliver Cromwell, politician and soldier (1599–1658)

Commitment to Excellence

What book is in your toilet? Does that sound like a weird question? If, like successful trader Matt Blom, you are committed to trading excellence, to becoming the best trader that you can be, and you are aware therefore of the need to keep learning and improving, then it may be *Market Wizards* or a similar trading book.

Matt is a very consistent, very successful trader, and apart from having an absolute passion for trading, he is extremely enthusiastic about how to become even better. He is always looking for ways of developing his trading style and strategy, of creating new edges in the market, of managing risk and improving his own trading ability as well as his psychology. Matt is committed to achieving personal and performance excellence and is focussed on continual improvement. This is a trait that I have noticed in many great traders, and indeed high performers in all areas. I think one of the most worrying phrases that I hear from traders is, "I've cracked it!"

"The quality of a person's life is in direct proportion to his commitment to excellence, regardless of his chosen field."

– Vince Lombardi, American Football coach

Adopt a Growth Mindset

Trading is an activity that presents continual learning and growth opportunities – but only for those traders who are ready to learn and to grow!

In her book *Mindset*, world-renowned Stanford University psychologist Carol Dweck, who spent decades researching achievement and success, had some interesting findings, which are excerpted overleaf.

In a fixed mindset, people believe their basic qualities, like their intelligence or talent, are simply fixed traits. They spend their time documenting their intelligence or talent instead of developing them. They also believe that talent alone creates success – without effort. They're wrong. In a growth mindset, people believe that their most basic abilities can be developed through dedication and hard work – brains and talent are just the starting point. This view creates a love of learning and a resilience that is essential for great accomplishment. Virtually all great people have had these qualities.

Mindsets are beliefs – beliefs about yourself and your most basic qualities. Think about your intelligence, your talents, your personality. Are these qualities simply fixed traits, carved in stone, and that's that? Or are they things you can cultivate throughout your life?

People with a fixed mindset believe that their traits are just givens. They have a certain amount of brains and talent and nothing can change that. If they have a lot, they're all set, but if they don't... So people in this mindset worry about their traits and how adequate they are. They have something to prove to themselves and others.

"Think about your intelligence, talents, and personality. Are they just fixed or can you develop them?"

People with a growth mindset, on the other hand, see their qualities as things that can be developed through their dedication and effort. Sure, they're happy if they're brainy or talented, but that's just the starting point. They understand that no one has ever accomplished great things – not Mozart, Darwin, or Michael Jordan – without years of passionate practice and learning.

– From *Mindset*, Carol Dweck, (Ballantine, 2007)

(Follow this address to a diagram of the fixed and growth mindset:

www.stanfordalumni.org/news/magazine/2007/marapr/images/features/dweck/dweck_mindset.pdf)

What Are the Implications for Traders?

For traders with a growth mindset, trading is a series of learning opportunities, of chances to grow as a trader as well as a person, to develop new skills, abilities, knowledge and understanding. It is driven by a desire to improve and become the best trader possible, fuelled by sustained effort and concentration. Feedback from each trade, trading day and trading period is seen as being important to development, and what some traders might perceive as failure, growth mindset traders see as feedback and opportunity to learn, develop and improve trading performance.

Traders with a growth mindset appreciate that trading is a skilled performance activity that requires practice and a developmental approach – trading is a unique activity and many people who start trading are not equipped mentally. It is common for these traders to be seen to be enjoying their trading, relishing the challenge of the markets, and focussing on the process of high quality trading alongside P&L, and, significantly, they are more likely to take responsibility for their trading outcomes.

> ❝ Traders with a growth mindset appreciate that trading is a skilled activity that requires a developmental approach. ❞

Some traders adopt more of a fixed mindset. Traders of this type are generally more ego and results-oriented and they can get consumed by P&L, due to being more focussed on outcomes rather than process. This desire to be right and to look good can have an adverse effect, in that breaking out of the comfort zone and achieving their full potential can be hampered by the fear of failure. This strong P&L focus can also lead to the trader breaking their strategy in an attempt to make money in other ways, focussing on short-term profits rather than long-term gain. Confidence can come and go, as P&L peaks and troughs.

These traders are less likely to adopt a developmental approach, incorporating aspects such as ongoing learning, training, coaching and mentoring, and are more likely to keep to what they know and are comfortable with. They are less flexible and open to change than growth mindset traders. Another key difference between the fixed mindset trader and the growth mindset trader is that the fixed mindset trader is more likely to blame others and complain about things – he takes less responsibility for his trading results.

So which type of trader are you? Do you have a fixed mindset or a growth mindset? If it is a fixed one, what could the benefits of adopting a more growth-focussed mindset be? And what would the impact on your trading be?

1. Acknowledge that trading is developmental and create a development programme for yourself (learning, reading, training, coaching, mentoring, etc). Ensure it is one that progresses over time, and is characterised by plenty of learning experiences and opportunities. Focus on who you need to become to achieve your trading goals.

2. No failure – only feedback; which is the "breakfast of champions" (Ken Blanchard and Spencer Johnson).

3. Focus on the process of trading – acquiring the relevant skills, knowledge and understanding and on the flawless execution of your strategy.

4. Take personal responsibility for your trading outcomes – ask, "How did I create that?"

5. Challenge yourself when you hear yourself saying "I can't do that...", or "that's not possible", or "that's how I am".

Development, Learning and Performance Improvement

If you wanted to learn to play golf, fly a plane, learn the piano, drive a car or how to cook what would you do? The majority of people would perhaps consider getting some lessons. If you wanted to become highly successful in those areas, then training and education would be probably foremost in your mind, followed, perhaps, by some coaching and mentoring as well.

It is no different with trading.

Training, coaching and mentoring *all* play a significant part in a trader's development.

Training

> "If I am through learning, I am through."
>
> **– John Wooden, legendary NCAA basketball coach**

Good quality intensive training is critical to achieving success in trading, just as it is in any other high-performance area. Training should be structured appropriately to meet the needs of the trader, and should have a relevant curriculum of study, with continuity and progression running throughout. Ideally there will be opportunities to practice, to try out ideas and learn the basics of execution on the simulator, and to trade live in the markets in real-time.

A key feature of all training programmes should be the opportunity to get regular feedback. This is the basis of quality learning experiences, and is powerful in accelerating development. The quality of a training programme can have a massive impact on the start of a trader's career, and can to a great extent either launch them onto the path of success or of failure.

For most traders, training typically occurs at the beginning of their careers and is formed around teaching the core basics, enabling the trader to engage in the markets with competence. However, it is useful to stay in the learning loop – to keep updating your market knowledge, to look at new trading methodologies, and to develop your psychology and performance skills.

Key aspects of a good quality training programme

- Relevant curriculum
- Continuity
- Progression
- Duration
- Feedback – regular and of a high quality
- Simulation
- Live trading
- Expert and experienced tutors with trading experience/success
- Assessment
- Lots of opportunities for interacting with the tutors
- Development post-training – mentoring/coaching opportunities

Mentoring

"I've seen good traders placed at the wrong desk, and they have done poorly (often leaving the trading profession). Similarly, I've seen bad traders survive longer than I would have thought possible, because they were mentored by someone who really cared about their development."

– Harold Cataquet, Cataquet and Associates Ltd

Mentoring is a process that goes right back in history and has stood the test of time as a very effective process of developing a person's competence in any given field.

Mentoring from a more experienced trader can be a very powerful experience when it is carried out correctly, and can have a significant positive impact on the speed and quality of your learning. Ideally, all trainee traders would be mentored. Thankfully many institutions have now realised its importance, and set up programmes accordingly.

The relationship between the mentor and the mentored has to be well defined, and both parties need to know what the aims and outcomes of the relationship are, and how the process will work. For the mentored, having someone to watch trade and to watch *them* trade, to bounce ideas and questions off, is extremely important. For the mentor, there are also benefits; I have seen that in mentoring someone, mentors have to consolidate their own understanding of what they are doing, develop very useful new skills in communication and self-awareness, get the immense satisfaction of watching students grow and develop. None of which should be sniffed at.

What to look for in a mentor

"Mentoring and coaching is very useful, but you should stick to just 1 or 2 such guides: otherwise you will get conflicting advice and confusion. Take this advice from people who actually trade and have done it, not from those who simply write commentaries or seminars."

– Shaun Downey

- Experience

- Knowledge

- Actual trading history

- Communication skills

- Commitment to students

- Time and availability

Interestingly, over time the mentored can become the mentor, as their skills and knowledge become greater, and are secured in a much more conscious, experienced and alert framework than is common. They are then sought out by other traders, and are able to pass on their experience. In my opinion, this is almost a natural part of the development of a real high-performance trader; and you would definitely be in the expert to master stages by this enviable point.

Real Life Examples: The Chain of Mentors

Ed Seykota realised a 250,000% return on his accounts over 16 years. "It is a happy circumstance that when nature gives us true burning desires, she also gives us the means to satisfy them. Those who want to win and lack skill can get someone with skill to help them."

Michael Marcus turned a $30,000 account into $80 million. "Then in October 1971, while at my broker's office, I met one of the people to whom I attribute my success – Ed Seykota. He is a genius and a great trader who has been phenomenally successful."

Bruce Kovner is a multi-billionaire. "Michael [Marcus] taught me one thing that was incredibly important ... He taught me that you could make a million dollars. He showed me that if you applied yourself, great things could happen."

Coaching

"Coaching for me provides focus and accountability; new perspectives and support. I can easily and truthfully say that the evidence shows that, for me, coaching enables me to lift my monthly P&L to about ten times that of when I am not in coaching."

– S.P., trader

In the trading and corporate arenas I define coaching as support and guidance that is not directly subject or content specific. So, in this case, anything that is not based around teaching trading skills or strategy. Subjects covered in this area might include performance coaching, psychological coaching or career coaching. The nature of these interventions is generally developmental and the process is designed to support the trader along their journey.

For many traders early on in their careers, the majority of the input is likely to be from training and mentoring, and focussed on developing the core skills, knowledge and understanding to actually trade.

Later on in their development the need may well become more focussed around performance and psychology, as they strive to achieve greater levels of performance and sustain them. I see this as being very similar in the sporting world, where at the early stages of an athlete's development the focus is on developing core skills, strategy and fitness; but as the athlete takes their physical performance to higher and higher levels, ultimately it is their mindset that becomes the critical factor between success and failure, and not their lack of mechanical skill.

Keep Raising the Bar

"Champions never ask whether or not it is possible to raise the bar on their performance. The question they ask is 'How is it possible; what do I have to do?'"

– Jerry Lynch, _The Way of the Champion_

In my experience as a coach and trainer in the sports, business, and trading arenas, I would say that about 80% of people come to coaching because they are having a tough time and are being reactive to events. They are struggling with their performance and looking for support to return to form. The other 20% are already performing well, but are proactively looking for ways in which they can further improve and raise their game.

From my perspective, coaching, training and mentoring only have one purpose – to raise performance levels, regardless of where that performance level currently sits. And that means that all traders can potentially benefit from the use of additional training, working with a mentor or getting coaching.

One of the key philosophies that I aim to pass on in my own training and coaching is LEARN more! Keep focussed on learning, because, as you *learn more*, so your potential to *earn more* grows. This might sound cheesy, but the evidence is inescapable.

Here are a few pointers to focus on to keep you learning

- Keep focussed on trying to do better than you currently are. Keep asking yourself, "How can I improve my trading performance? What do I have to do?"

- Keep taking small steps forward – do not underestimate the power of taking many small steps!

- Be teachable and coachable – be open to new experiences, to new ideas and concepts. Socrates said, "My wisdom lay in this; unlike other men I knew how ignorant I was."

Practical Strategy: Ensuring Continual Development

The most important factor in ensuring continual development is that you adopt it as a mindset – as a part of your trading philosophy. Committing to continual improvement is a reflection of the beliefs and attitudes that you hold – adopt a growth mindset!

Stay in the performance cycle – plan, execute and evaluate, and use the feedback from your evaluations to drive performance improvements

Keep focussed on learning – ask yourself regularly, "What have I learnt? What do I need to know now? What action do I need to take?"

Keep assessing your trading development needs and read, research or attend training courses to fulfil that need. Regularly ask yourself, "What three specific things that I am not doing now would definitely contribute to improving my current performance level?"

Consider getting a mentor to work with.

Psychological and performance coaching. If you are having specific psychological challenges with your trading, or want support with raising the level of your existing trading performance, then these can be very useful too.

STRATEGY 26

Know Your Score – Measuring Trading Performance

"It is important for traders to keep their own score – to give
accountability and responsibility."

– Nick Shannon, occupational psychologist

E valuation and analysis is critical to achieving your full potential as a trader. Post-performance it is essential to record what has happened, and to evaluate your performance. It is a key component of the performance cycle.

Trade logs, daily evaluation and keeping journals are recognised by all trading coaches and trading psychologists as being critical to improving performance. Evaluation is, however, often underrated by traders; with most time being consumed with execution, and maybe some beforehand on planning and preparation. But your trading metrics and results are a reflection of your trading behaviour – they will leave many clues as to what you have done well and where you can improve. Most importantly, too, they are *objective* – the numbers are the numbers, and are not prone to the psychological biases that interfere with our subjective evaluations.

What else can we measure?

Well, after outcome, we can look at performance measures. In sport these include the types of statistics you might expect, depending on the activity: unforced errors, putts per round, fouls, telemetry. In trading, aspects such as the number of ticks/pips made, the number of and percentage of winners/losers, round turns/commissions, the average winner and loser, etc, can all be good performance measures – or, as they are often termed, *metrics.*

The advantage of looking at performance measures such as these is that our ability to alter them is then placed far more under our control. They are essentially the components of the outcome.

Example Performance Metrics

- Number of trades placed

- Number and/or percentage of winners/losers

- Average winner (monetary amount)

- Average loser (monetary amount)

- Average winner/average loser

- Number of longs vs. shorts

- Average time in trade

- Time of day and number of trades placed

- Expectancy (% of winners x average winner) – (% of losers x average loser)

What else can we measure? Well, at the opposite end of the outcome is the process. What is covered in the process? In sport it would include the application of tactics, maintaining positive psychology, nutritional strategies, warming up and cooling down, focus on performance of particular skills, etc. In trading, this would cover aspects such as preparation and planning, evaluation, trade logs, energy management, emotional state control, trade entry, management and exits, etc. Process goals are the most controllable aspect of our performance, and the least widely used and considered in trading. Identifying the key processes of trading well, and then monitoring and measuring them, can be an excellent way of improving performance over time.

Developing Your Own Trading Evaluation Process

There is a great phrase that says *what gets measured gets done*. Once you begin to measure your performance you will naturally want to improve it.

What aspects of your trading can you begin to measure? How and when will you assess them?

Take some time to consider your performance and process measures, put them in place, monitor and assess them, and then decide on what time frame you will review them; perhaps a mixture of daily, weekly and monthly, dependent on the time frames you trade and the number of trades you place.

Interestingly, one of the arguments, or barriers, that traders often put in the way of keeping trade logs, or evaluating their trading, is the time it takes. But evaluation does not have to be time-consuming, with the use of spreadsheets and computers. However, there is a time requirement, or rather, a time *investment*. Time spent in evaluating is an investment in that it helps to develop and improve performance, and therefore P&L. It tells you in numerical terms how you are actually performing, which can be different to how you think you are doing! It can help you to identify patterns, both useful and limiting, in your trading, which if acted upon will impact positively on your profitability.

Practical Strategy: Designing Your Trading Evaluation Process

Decide on what you will measure – what will be useful for you to know about your trading?

Decide on how you will capture the data.

Decide on the time frame by which you will evaluate.

Sample Performance Analysis/Evaluation Headings

- Outcome: P&L
- Performance metrics
- Trader processes
- Market conditions
- Summative evaluation
- What has gone well?
- Where are the areas for improvement?
- What action will be taken?

What Should I Log?

There are many possible trading metrics and aspects that you can log and evaluate.

For your trade log you may wish to consider:

- Trade entry – market; position size; long/short; time and reasons for entry
- Trade exit – market; position size; long/short; time and reasons for exit
- Trade management – did you add to or reduce your position? Size; long/short/time(s) and reasons for doing so
- Summative evaluation of the trade noting any key points

Some core areas to consider for a longer-term (end of day/week – this will all depend on your trading frequency) journal might be:

- Profit and loss
- Trades made/round trips

- Number of winners vs. losers

- Average winner and loser

- Biggest winner and loser

- Performance processes – how well did you execute your strategy? Were you disciplined? How was your risk and money management? How were you mentally/emotionally?

- Market conditions – how did the market trade? What was the volatility like? Volumes? Range? Were there any economic releases, speakers, auctions, etc?

- Feedback – What went well? Where could you improve? Any key points of learning? What action will you take as a result?

Conduct Periodic Trading Reviews

It is extremely useful periodically to conduct a review of your trading. Looking at your trading data over a large time period will give you a far greater sample size and greater reliability when you come to perform your analysis – this is even more important if you trade less frequently, as over a day, week, month or even longer there may be little data to review.

The time frame of such a review is largely down to the trader, their trading style and particular frequency. In general, with active traders I will often use a monthly review as standard, with a more in-depth one either quarterly or annually. For less active traders, maybe a quarterly review is more appropriate.

I have provided here a simple format (some of which may be more relevant than others – take away what is useful for you) that you can use to conduct a trading review. Once you have conducted the review, then the most important step is to generate your goals and outcomes for the upcoming trading period (see STRATEGY 5).

Practical Strategy: Conducting a Periodic Review

Look over your trading metrics for the period and collate them

Measures to consider

- Gross P&L over the period

- Net P&L over the period

- Costs of trading – commissions; facilities

- Number of trades placed

- Number and percentage (success rate) of Winners: Losers: Scratches

- Total profits made over the period

- Total losses made over the period

- Biggest winner/loser

- Average winner/loser (pay off ratio)

- Consecutive winners and losers

- Biggest period of drawdown

Choose up to 10 metrics/measures to analyse your trading with and enter them into the table below

Key Trading Metrics for Period

Metric/KPI	Value

Comments/observations on your metrics (what do you notice?)

Look over your trading metrics (you may like to identify some as your Key Performance Indicators – KPIs) and analyse them – what story do they tell? It can also be useful here to cross-reference them against historical data, particularly if you have averages for them.

Complete the questions below fully and honestly

What were your key achievements (performance and results)?

What evidence of progress is there?

What did you do well?

What are the key areas for improvement?

What did you learn?

What are your key trading goals and objectives for the next period?

(contd.)

What are the key points of your strategy/action plan for achieving your goals for the next period?

Consider

What should you do more of?

What should you do less of?

What should you start doing?

What should you stop doing?

What help/support/resources do you need to achieve those goals/objectives?

STRATEGY 27

Develop Winning Routines and Rituals

"We are what we repeatedly do. Excellence then is not an act
but a habit."

– Aristotle

Routines and Rituals

Exercise: The Benefits of Habit

Write down everything that you did from the moment you woke up, until 0900 this morning.

Is this similar to what you do on most days?

Do you have breakfast and then shower or shower and then breakfast? Do you always get up at the same time? Do you always press the snooze button – how many times?

How does what you do benefit you?

Most people have some kind of morning routine. This has been developed by them over the years, primarily to get them to the state they need to be in to go about the rest of their day effectively. The process of developing this may not have been conscious – they have adapted it and refined it over time, based on experience. And their day, right up until they go to bed, will be filled with such embedded routines.

Routines can be very powerful. We all have certain rituals that we repeat on a daily basis, both consciously and unconsciously, and some can be traced back to events as early as primary school – having been merely in development or adjustment ever since. Routines and rituals can enable us to quickly and efficiently get ready to *do*; to get into the required state for action, with the minimum of worry. If you watch a pro-golfer they will have a pre-shot routine that allows them to get into the right mental and physical shape to hit the golf ball. Actors, singers and dancers often go through a pre-performance ritual, as do people giving presentations. It is natural, then, that we should do so every day in trading; and even more natural that we should seek to enhance *how* we do so, in working towards high performance.

Can you think of some of your existing pre-performance routines? What actions and thoughts do you go through, for example, before giving a presentation? Going into an exam/test? Going for an interview? Before playing sport?

As a trader it can be very useful to establish some core routines for yourself – dependent on your own preferences you may wish to have a lot of very rigid routines or less and a more flexible approach. Either way there are significant benefits to establishing some.

Goal of Rituals: Create Consistency

"Consistency is in the mind, not the markets."

– Mark Douglas, *The Disciplined Trader*

What is consistency in trading?

"I would like greater consistency in my trading."

This is one of the most common phrases I hear in my work with traders. The first question that I will ask them is to define what they mean by consistency. So what does consistency mean to you?

If it means making absolutely the same amount of money every day, week, month or year, then this may be an extremely challenging (and, in many respects, arbitrary) goal for you to achieve.

In most cases the trader wants some form of consistent profits from their trading, without any periods of drawdown, or flat months or weeks. Is this possible? Maybe, and there are certainly some traders who have quite consistent levels of P&L returns. However, for the majority of traders it is simply not the case, and the key reason for this is the interplay of the trader with the markets. If a trader is making £X per period when there are ten tradeable opportunities, then it would be unrealistic to expect them to make £X again when there are only five tradeable opportunities (all other things remaining equal, e.g. position sizing).

The number of opportunities and the nature of those opportunities does, therefore, have some impact on P&L, and to a degree this means that as traders we need to go with the flow a little – accepting that there will be P&L fluctuations.

Consistency in trading, then, is much more a case of consistency in the way that you *think, feel and behave.* This is part of the value of having routines for preparation, evaluation, and so on. Because the markets are largely out of our control, we cannot guarantee consistency of returns. However, what we can do is to recognise those elements of trading that are controllable by us, and to focus on gaining consistency in these aspects.

Avoid Negative Rituals

Of course, it is possible to have routines or rituals that are not conducive to performance – these are known as maladaptive or negative rituals, and often these can restrict performance, remove our desired level of self-control and even cause illness. For example, when drugs or alcohol are used as a ritual for rest and relaxation, the impact can be extreme: such practices must be avoided at all costs. As a trader, large volumes of stress require systematic sessions of *recovery*, not obliteration, to prevent overstraining or burnout. This shall be covered in the development of positive rituals discussed below.

Establish Positive Rituals

In *Stress for Success* by James E. Loehr, the following ten areas are identified as being the most important to develop successful rituals in: whether to regulate, calm, bolster, energise or clarify things for the trader or professional.

- Sleep – consistent patterns for getting up and going to bed protect the sleep cycle. Going to bed early and waking up early works for most performers.

- Exercise – daily exposure to exercise of some kind is critical to overall balance.

- Nutrition – the timing, frequency and content of your meals is extremely important.

- Family – time with family grounds you, creates bonds and affirms meaning in your life.

- Spirituality – spiritual time heals you, confirming your purpose and essentials in life – a foundation for personal growth.

- Pre-performance – like tennis players and golfers before serving or putting, traders need precise preparation routines before trading.

- Travel – to gain control over your emotional response to traffic or train on your commute to the office, build a ritual around it.

- Office – the in-between time in trading is critical to success. It's time for recovery and then preparation. Taking small 'carbo-breaks' such as an apple; leaving your desk for a walk around – fresh air, even a walk up and down a flight of stairs; then allowing yourself a few minutes for your pre-prep ritual before you begin your next trade!

- Creative time – playing a musical instrument, creative writing, artistic pursuits, etc, all play a critical role in balancing stress.

- Home – creating home-rituals to wind down after a day's trading (oscillating) reenergises and is just as important as getting psyched or being fired up to perform.

Practical Strategy: Devising Your Own Trading Performance and Lifestyle Rituals

Reflect on your current trading performance and lifestyle. Make a list of any routines and rituals that you already have.

Now go through your list and identify any that may be maladaptive/negative and identify those that are positive and performance-enhancing.

For any maladaptive rituals that you have, ask yourself what purpose they serve you, and see if you can find a more positive way in which to serve that same purpose. For example, if you drink alcohol (in greater than moderation!) to relax, is there some other way in which you could achieve relaxation but that is healthier?

Keep any established positive rituals.

Consider rituals and routines that you do not already have that would enhance your performance or your lifestyle and make a list of these. Over time gradually implement your new rituals – build slowly allowing you to establish and condition the ritual without getting overwhelmed by trying to do too many new things at once.

STRATEGY 28

Build Resilience

"I can think of no psychological characteristic more important to long-term trading success than psychological resilience. Resilience has been defined in a number of ways, sometimes as a process, other times as a trait. In all cases, resilience presumes exposure to stressful conditions and an ability to maintain high levels of social, emotional, and vocational functioning throughout this exposure. My experience with traders suggests that even the most successful ones go through periods of drawdown. Sometimes these drawdowns are extended, either in time or in the amount of money lost. Some traders bounce back from these losses; others don't."

– Brett Steenbarger, traderblogspot.com

What is Resilience?

In demanding situations there can be great pressure and adversity. In these situations you can either dive, survive or thrive! At best we want to be able to strive, to remain competent and perform well, to prevent, minimise or overcome any possible damaging effects and eventually – by going through this process and being exposed to such challenges – to adapt and be strengthened by our experiences.

At worst we want to survive – to get through the period with the minimum damage done!

Our least desirable outcome is to dive, to crumble under the pressure, to fail to adapt, to give up or to just get beaten down.

Resilience is the capacity to survive or thrive in adversity with the experience of unfortunate or stressful events such as in trading losses, setbacks and errors.

"Mental toughness is judged by the speed in which a trader can recover from losses and mistakes within a trading session; how quickly they recover from larger losses; and the ability to continue trading while going through a prolonged period of losses or bad performance, and then eventually turn things around."

– Tariq Arees, trader

Why is it Important?

Because trading is a demanding endeavour. Trading presents you with much challenge, pressure and often adversity. Traders lose, they make mistakes, they encounter tough periods in the market, they go through drawdown and they have setbacks. And this happens to *all* traders, not simply the unsuccessful; the key to success, then, is not to avoid this, but to bounce back from it. Winners suffer, but they endure. They have resilience. It is the deciding factor.

Exercise: Resiliency Rating Self-Assessment

Answer each one of the following statements as either *true* or *false*.

- I have future goals which I feel motivated and excited about achieving.

- I find it easy to get going again after setbacks, losses or errors.

- I don't give up when progress is slow or get put off achieving an objective by tasks I find boring or unpleasant.

- I find creative ways of rising to challenges.

- Under pressure I rarely feel helpless or fatigued.

- I don't let difficult periods, with few wins, affect my confidence.

- When challenged, I am able to summon a wide range of positive emotions to engage my fighting spirit and maintain a sense of humour.

- I know how to motivate myself under adverse conditions.

- If I start out badly, it's easy for me to turn my performance around.

- I see slumps in performance as temporary.

The more *true* answers you have, the greater your resilience. Total up the number of times you have answered *true* and then multiply by 10 to get a percentage score e.g. 6 True = 60%. This is your current Resiliency Rating.

Make a note of your rating and also the areas where you answered *false*. These are key areas for development. Which one if you could change the answer to a *true* do you feel would have the biggest positive impact on your trading performance? Make this your primary resiliency development goal. Read through the suggestions within this chapter (and also look throughout the book for related topics) and find a practical strategy to implement.

The Three Components of Resilience

I like to think of resilience in trading as being composed of three parts:

1. Financial resilience

2. Physical resilience

3. Psychological resilience

Resilience as a trader depends upon a combination of all three aspects. Your financial resilience (financial situation) and your physical resilience (energy) will both have an affect on your psychological resilience (mental and emotional toughness).

In developing a high level of resilience you should seek to develop all three areas and not just focus on psychological resilience or mental toughness.

Financial Resilience

"The biggest obstacle to trading success is financial constraint, in my humble opinion. Most traders believe in their ability to pick more winning trades than losers; however it is finances that can dictate their conviction with them. If a trader has limited capital it will ultimately cause them to bail out of trades if they begin to look like they could be a loser and can also cause them to snatch at profits when on the upside (I have done this plenty). I truly believe if the majority of traders had unlimited capital they would prove a lot more profitable, just because of the sense of security it brings."

– Lawrie Inman, Trader

Finances are rarely thought of when resilience is discussed – however, in my view, they are an absolutely fundamental part of trading resilience. If resilience is about being able to weather tough patches in the market, to be able to bounce back to be able to keep going and stay in the game, then having a sufficient supply of capital is absolutely critical. In fact for me, financial resilience may in fact be the most important component of trader resilience.

Financial resilience has three levels to it:

1. *Personal capital/wealth* – your personal level of financial wealth. This is important because if in trading you encounter difficult periods and challenges then trading may not be able to pay you what you would like or need. If you have sufficient personal capital then during such periods you will be able survive without the need to go into desperation mode trying to make money to pay bills etc. This can have a significant impact on the success or failure of a trader. Additionally, for people who are trading their own account your trading capital will be allocated from your personal wealth. If your trading capital is a large proportion of your personal wealth then every loss impacts at two levels – your trading account and your personal wealth; and that increases the pain and the emotional impact of a loss.

2. *Trading capital* – the allocation of capital you have to trade with. The size of your trading capital is most significant because it is a determinant of the size that you can trade and the positions that you can take. If your trading capital is small then either you accept this and take small risks and receive small rewards or if you are trying to make big returns on that capital then you are essentially forced into taking large risks. Obviously taking large and excessive risks is not desirable but for most people neither is making small returns – greed and expectations that are greater than your trading capital will in most cases end up in a trading style is that high risk, with high volatility of wins and losses and ultimately a highly emotional and in most cases negative and unprofitable experience. Having a good base of trading capital allows you to take risk that is appropriate *and* returns you achievable P&L results.

3. *Risk taken* – the amount of risk you take in the markets is a feature of you, your trading style and the amount of trading capital you have. Regardless of the size of your trading capital there will be a finite amount of contracts that you can trade as determined by your risk manger or broker. However, how much of these limits you decide to use and how big the positions you decide to take are down to you. In lots of trading books they talk about taking 1-2% risk in terms of your position size. Every trader has to find a style and methodology that is appropriate for them, their trading strategy and the markets they are trading. However it is important to note that excessive risk taking can be detrimental to making good decisions, can elevate stress levels and be a cause of fear and anxiety in traders.

Your risk taken, trading capital and personal capital should all be linked and related to each other. For people trading their own accounts the model may essentially form a pyramid: personal capital being the base, trading capital a smaller portion of that and then trading size a smaller portion of that. For institutional traders, the trading capital and sizing relationship will be similar – however, personal capital due to the difference in pay and conditions and capital allocation structure may not be quite the same.

> ### Exercise: Financial Resilience Assessment
>
> Take a moment to assess your financial resilience.
>
> Are you financially strong? Could you weather a tough period in the markets and still bounce back?
>
> How long could you survive with no trading income?
>
> What percentage of your trading capital are you risking every trade? How many losses could you incur at this rate?

Physical Resilience

I am sure we can all think of a time when we felt run down, low in energy and noticed how our mood had changed for the worst – perhaps you were more irritable or impatient, or less focussed? Imagine how this can impact on your trading.

The second component of resilience is physical resilience, essentially having the energy to cope with everything. When trading is tough, and it can be very tough, it takes a lot out of you physically as well as mentally and emotionally. Your body is producing adrenaline on the highs and cortisol as you get stressed. The production and recycling of both of these takes energy away from you – it is a withdrawal from the energy bank. The longer this period goes on the more you withdraw until eventually you go overdrawn and then bust! The higher your energy bank level is to begin with the more withdrawals you can withstand and if you are able to make some energy deposits along the way to top up then obviously that has a big impact too. So having a good bank of physical energy and being able to top it up is important.

When you are physically run down your body lacks the energy to mobilise the high-energy emotional states it needs to operate and produce your Ideal Trading States – motivation, challenge, confidence, focus and concentration. Because you are low in energy your mood is affected and most people find that they make more mistakes, get irritated, angry or frustrated more easily and lose motivation and the desire to bounce back and perform in this state.

The diagram shows the core components of developing a physical resilience and by ensuring that these areas are covered and topped up regularly you can build a good energy bank account – for more information on developing your physical resilience go to STRATEGY 14, where the management of physical energy is discussed in detail.

Psychological Resilience

Psychological resilience is a mindset – it is about how you mentally deal with tough situations; what you chose to think and say to yourself in those events and what beliefs, attitudes and perceptions you have that underpin them.

The diagram below shows how the mindset of a trader operates. An activating event such as a loss is filtered through the trader's mindset in terms of their beliefs, attitudes, perceptions and son; this generates a feeling and a set of subsequent behaviours and actions; which is then is played out in the trader's performance. The activating event can be the same for many different traders and yet the outcomes could all be vastly different based on their mindset. It is therefore not the events that happen to us that actually determine our results, but rather, as we looked at in the chapter on personal responsibility, ourselves – in this case, our mindset.

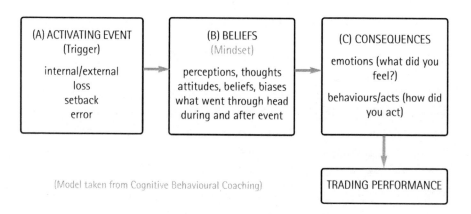

(A) ACTIVATING EVENT (Trigger)	(B) BELIEFS (Mindset)	(C) CONSEQUENCES
internal/external loss setback error	perceptions, thoughts attitudes, beliefs, biases what went through head during and after event	emotions (what did you feel?) behaviours/acts (how did you act)

(Model taken from Cognitive Behavioural Coaching)

TRADING PERFORMANCE

There are many different models and ways in which to develop resilience psychologically and we are going to explore three of them now. I have chosen these ones based on the responses I have had from the traders I have worked with and also the ease in which they can be understood and implemented with good effect.

1. Beliefs, attitudes, perceptions and meaning

Your beliefs, attitudes and perceptions of what losses, setbacks and errors are will all have a big impact on how you react to them; they are a filtering mechanism for the actual event to go through before thoughts and emotions are experienced, and eventually actions are triggered.

Write down your beliefs, thoughts and attitudes about losses, setbacks and errors.

What is a loss? What does it mean to you?

What is a setback? What does it mean to you?

What is an error? What does it mean to you?

Examine your beliefs and look for ones that are empowering and useful – that provide resilience. Look for ones that are limiting, that are not useful, and commit to changing them.

Below are some sample positive beliefs that will help to generate resilience to losses, setbacks and errors:

It is OK to make mistakes – trading is not a game of perfection!

Setbacks are natural, as are plateaus in performance development.

A losing trade or run does not mean 'I am a loser'.

A mistake is an opportunity to learn.

Setbacks are a chance to review and reflect and get ready to move forward.

Losses are a part of trading – they are just an outcome.

2. Perspective

Perspective can be very powerful. How we choose to look at events can have a big impact on how we feel about them. Two useful perspectives that you can take to help to deal with adverse events more effectively are the 'wide lens' and the 'long lens'.

The wide lens encourages you to take a wider perspective to look at what you can take out of the event other than the result. A useful question to activate the wide lens is 'What can I learn from this?' Looking at what you can learn rather than just dwelling on the outcome shifts your perspective, encourages a different level of thinking and generates new possibilities for future outcomes.

> "I have missed more than 9000 shots in my career. I have lost almost 300 games. On 26 occasions I have been entrusted to take the game winning shot... and I missed. I have failed over and over and over again in my life. And that's precisely why I succeed."
>
> – Michael Jordan

There are lessons in every loss, setback or error – they are learning opportunities. If there has been a financial loss then this can be seen as a cost of learning, and can then be invested in making future returns by not repeating the mistake or error. This is taking a wide lens view.

The long lens encourages you to take perspective from a different point in time in the future; to look back on events of the past and to see how you would view them. This enables you to put matters into a time-based perspective. In the moment, and in the immediate future, events can appear very different to when looking back on them in a few months' time, and the level of emotional intensity is also likely to reduce as time goes on. I like to use a six-month lens, but you can use three, nine, twelve or even longer if needed.

Practical Strategy: Changing Perspective

Think of a loss/setback/error you have encountered – look at it with a wide lens – 'What can I learn from this?' – what do you notice?

Think of a loss/setback/error you have encountered – look at it with a long lens – go six months into the future and imagine looking back on the event – what do you notice?

3. Self-talk: explanatory style

Cognitive psychologists suggest that an individual's explanatory style can be a significant factor in influencing their level of performance. The research done by Martin Seligman (*Learned Optimism*, 1990) suggests that individuals with an optimistic explanatory style not only consistently outperform those with a pessimistic explanatory style but are also happier and live longer. Seligman's work is essentially based on attribution theory, which is the study of how people explain good and bad events that happen in their lives. An individual's explanatory style can be used to determine their level of optimism or pessimism.

Seligman's work covered three core dimensions which, it has been suggested, determine optimism or pessimism, and whether events are ultimately positive or negative to a person.

- Personalisation (Ps) – how personally people take events

- Permanence (Pm) – the time factor to which the person dwells on the event

- Pervasiveness (Pv) – how contextually or globally the person makes the event

Researchers suggest that an optimistic explanatory style, particularly about bad events, encourages perseverance: pessimistic people are more likely to lose confidence and motivation after a poor performance than optimists, and encouraging optimism in traders can therefore bolster resilience. With pessimistic traders, when a negative event occurs – for example, a big loss; a sustained period of drawdown; making an error; and so on – then their explanatory style would promote less perseverance, and maybe result in those traders not achieving their full potential.

"It's significant to note that one can't *not* make explanations about the events that happen in one's life; one has to do that in order to make meaning out of the world. However, the consequences of the type of explanations one makes is very different. If we tend to make more optimistic explanations about events, then we'll be more successful in the long run, than if we tend to make more pessimistic explanations."

— Jeffrey Hodges, Sportsmind

Practical Strategy: Building Resilience – Getting Tough!

Develop your financial resilience. Ensure that you have a positive relationship between personal capital, trading capital and size traded.

Maintain as high a positive physical energy bank as is possible by focussing on your sleep, nutrition, exercise and recovery.

Become strong mentally by developing positive resilient beliefs, taking empowering perspectives of events and by practising an optimistic explanatory style.

STRATEGY 29

Manage Stress

"Stress is when you wake up screaming and realise you haven't fallen asleep yet."

– Unknown

Stress and Trading

Trading is a results-driven occupation where you are dealing constantly with uncertainty and risk, and where there are major consequences to the decisions you make. All of these combined can make trading stressful. It cannot be escaped, as it is produced by elements intrinsic to trading; so we have to accept it and consider how to best manage it, as we move towards high performance.

What is Stress?

The first thing to clarify is that, unlike pressure, stress is never good for you, and never a positive thing. Stress creates unhealthy biological reactions, and prolonged stress can lead to both physical and mental health breakdown. This has often been referred to as *burnout*.

The Health and Safety Executive (HSE) define stress as, "the adverse reaction people have to excessive pressure or other types of demand placed upon them."

Stress is often defined as, and occurs when, the perceived demands that a person is under exceed the resources they have to cope with those demands.

What is the Difference Between Stress and Pressure?

There is very little difference between stress and pressure other than having adequate resources to cope with the demand placed on you. Perhaps this is why so many people talk of positive stress, when really they mean positive pressure.

Stress is an adverse response to what an individual perceives as too much pressure and can result from being under high pressure over extended periods of time. Essentially stress is not good for you. Stress is an unhealthy state of body or mind, or both, and can result in severe medical conditions. It is no coincidence that 'distress' contains the same term.

People often talk about the *flight or fight* response as being the stress response, but flight/fight is a one-off reaction to a perceived challenge or pressure, and is not necessarily bad for the individual. In some cases it is very helpful. It is good to be alerted to possible threats and to prepare to take evasive action. However, continually being in this state means that the body chemicals associated with flight/fight are then constantly being stimulated, and the result is ill-health of one type or another. This is stress or distress.

Signs and Symptoms of Stress?

How do you know if you are stressed? What are the signs and symptoms to look for?

These are some of the symptoms that are indicators of pressure-beyond-resources, which come from yourself, work, home, or any combination of the three. It is really useful to think back to times when you have been under impossible pressure, when you have been genuinely *stressed*, and to think about what signs and symptoms you displayed. Knowing the difference between when you are under pressure and when you are under stress is a very useful level of awareness to have. It is particularly good if you can identify the early warning signs, the first signs and symptoms that stress is setting in.

1. Psychological signs

- Inability to concentrate or make simple decisions
- Memory lapses
- Easily distracted
- Less intuitive & creative
- Worrying
- Negative thinking
- Depression & anxiety
- Emotional signs
- Tearful
- Irritable
- Mood swings
- Extra sensitive to criticism

- Defensive

- Feeling out of control

- Lack of motivation

- Angry

- Frustrated

- Lack of confidence

- Lack of self-esteem

2. Physical signs

- Aches/pains & muscle tension/grinding teeth

- Frequent colds/infections

- Allergies/rashes/skin irritations

- Constipation/diarrhoea/IBS

- Weight loss or gain

- Indigestion/heartburn/ulcers

- Hyperventilating/lump in the throat/pins & needles

- Dizziness/palpitations

- Panic attacks/nausea

- Physical tiredness

- Menstrual changes/loss of libido/sexual problems

- Heart problems/high blood pressure

3. Behavioural signs

- No time for relaxation or pleasurable activities

- Prone to accidents, forgetfulness

- Increased reliance on alcohol, smoking, caffeine, recreational or illegal drugs

- Becoming a workaholic

- Poor time management and/or poor standards of work

- Absenteeism

- Self-neglect/change in appearance

- Social withdrawal

- Relationship problems

- Insomnia or waking tired

- Reckless

- Aggressive/anger outbursts

- Nervous

- Uncharacteristically lying

The symptoms that affect you will often build up over time, until you are forced to take notice of them. Keep a check on how you are feeling and behaving and 'check in' to see whether you are beginning to show any signs of stress. It is often the behavioural symptoms that are noticed, especially by other people, as they are more obvious. It is vital that you don't rationalise the symptoms away; and if you are at all concerned or unsure about any, see a doctor.

Stress, Pressure and Performance

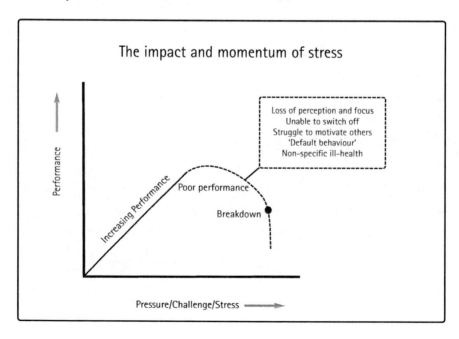

The impact and momentum of stress

The diagram on p.248 is based on the Yerkes-Dodson curve and shows the relationship between pressure, stress and performance. As we get increasing pressure, performance is also enhanced – up to the point where the coping capacity of the individual is less than the demands of the task. At this point, performance turns and begins to decline. If the pressure continues over time, then stress occurs, performance continues to decline quite rapidly, and ill health awaits.

A very important factor in performing well under pressure and in coping with stress is to know where your 'tipping point' is – in reality it is more of a zone – and to be aware of where you are at any given time on the curve. If you are spending lots of time on the left, then you may well be underperforming, and may be experiencing lack of challenge and boredom – which, interestingly, can also be very stressful. If you are spending all of your time on the right, then you really need to be aware that you are in the stress zone; and you should try your utmost to move to the left a little more.

Build Your Stress Capacity

"I have learnt that stress is never the real enemy. Protection from stress never took these athletes where they wanted to go. To the contrary, success was always linked to the same two things – stress exposure and stress response."

– James E. Loehr, *Stress for Success*

As said, trading is a pressurised activity, so it is not possible to take away or eliminate performance stress from it entirely without giving up trading! In *Stress for Success*, James E. Loehr reiterates the fact that in many top-performing activities, high pressure and stressful situations are a part of those environments, and that stress reduction is not really a viable strategy. Loehr suggests an approach that builds a person's resilience and ability to cope more effectively with the pressure and stress that they are encountering.

This is done by a process of exposure to the stressful events, and then recovery. During the recovery process there is a process of overcompensation that occurs, that prepares you to engage again but with a higher stress threshold. This is the same process as how you grow muscle. You go to the gym and do your weight training – that's the exposure. Then you rest, let the muscle recover and grow – that's the overcompensation and increasing of capacity (you are stronger!)

Increased stress exposure + quality recovery = greater stress capacity

Increasing stress exposure is a natural process that occurs on most good graduate programmes. The level of demand is raised slowly over time, allowing the students to develop their resilience to a new level.

Reducing Trading Stress

There are some things that you can do to make trading a little less stressful or to keep the stress to the expected levels, including:

- Taking appropriate risk – big positions beyond your financial threshold create stress!

- Setting realistic goals and expectations – expectations and pressure

- Preparation

- Accept that losses, risk and uncertainty are a part of trading

- Match challenge and capability

- Work within, or stretch, your limits – be careful about pushing on too far

- Trade don't gamble – trade your strategy!

Practical Strategies: Managing Stress

Here are eight strategies for helping you to manage stress and deal with the pressures of trading in the first place.

1. Accept that trading has pressure and potential stress.

2. Be aware of where you are on the stress, pressure, performance curve. Be really attentive if you are finding that you are spending a long time at either end of the curve – these are the danger zones! Watch out for 'distress' – prolonged stress will lead to burnout and ill-health.

3. Build your stress exposure over time through gradually building the demands of your trading – slowly increasing your position sizing, complexity of trades, diversification, etc.

4. Take appropriate steps to ensure that you are not making your trading more stressful than it has to be.

5. Manage stress by looking after yourself physically – NERS yourself – Nutrition, Exercise, Relaxation and Sleep (STRATEGY 14)

6. Get balance in your life – friends, family, hobbies, interests – create a diverse personal portfolio

7. Laugh! Humour is a very powerful state manager. The endorphins released when we laugh make us feel great.

8. Learn to relax. Relaxation is a very positive and powerful state to enter. When you are deeply relaxed, you are entering a restorative state where your mind and body can recover. Using relaxation techniques can potentially be a great way of dealing with stress.

 Trader Top Tips

"I've had very little stress in the business but I do have periods where I get angry with myself and use language that is embarrassing at times to say the least. Fortunately, it doesn't happen often but when it does I know that it is my way of releasing stress and I try to bounce back and laugh about the experience."

– Larry Pasavento, hedge fund manager

"Get involved in activities outside of work so you have some form of release and can clear your head."

– Tony Dicarlo, trader

"You need a way to deal with stress. Exercise is a common method, but something as simple as taking five deep breaths in and out is incredibly effective when events just seem to be piling up on top of you."

– Harold Cataquet, Cataquet and Associates

STRATEGY 30

Achieve Balance

"Trading is 24/7 for the first two years at least – and then you can get some balance."

– Lex Van Dam, hedge fund manager

Balance vs. Immersion

Trading is one of those activities that is positively *consuming*, and can become life rather than just a part of it. As a full-time occupation it is more than a job. As a hobby or part-time occupation it is more than a job! Traders tend to trade the markets all day, and then many spend time socialising with other traders and talking about the markets, before going to bed and dreaming about the markets! Does that sound familiar?

Being committed to and passionate about trading is a key requisite to success, and in the early days of a trader's career, in particular, the need to immerse yourself into your chosen profession and to 'get the hours in' is actually pretty critical to success. At one of the trading organisations where I work, graduate traders are encouraged to not take any holiday inside the first seven months – they are expected to be there every day for ten to twelve hours at a time, immersing themselves in the markets, getting as much exposure and experience as is possible. However, getting some balance – and, importantly, rest and recovery – is also an important part of keeping your perspective, and critically your health, in good shape!

The Importance of Rest and Recovery

"Consistent performance is achieved when you have a healthy oscillation between positive peak performance states, and periods of recovery."

– James E. Loehr, *Stress for Success*

Seeking regular and valuable recovery throughout our practice as traders renews our energy and allows us to become more fully engaged in what we are doing. The process of alternating periods of stress or pressure, followed by periods of recovery, is what James E. Loehr in his book *Stress for Success* refers to as oscillation. If you keep something continually under stress, then eventually it will break – this is akin to overuse injuries and overtraining in sports, where people keep training and training but with no recovery periods.

Take a Break!

Ollie was a day trader who was very successful, but was experiencing difficult times with his trading. Over the last few months his performance had declined, and he had come to coaching for some guidance and support. It was July, and Ollie told me that he had three weeks holiday booked in August – but that he was thinking of cancelling it to stay and try and make some money instead.

He felt that it would be wrong to go away with his trading account being where it was, and that he should focus on his trading and not his poolside relaxation. But it was obvious from his tone, body language and apparent lack of energy and enthusiasm that what Ollie needed more than anything was a holiday. He had not had a break for almost a year, and had been full-on in the markets. This, combined with the tough time he was having, was really taking it out of him.

We sat and we talked about his feelings of needing to stay and make money, his desire to focus on his trading versus his obvious need to get away to some greatly needed rest and recovery, in order to come back to the markets enthused, fresh and energised. It all stems from a problem many traders face – there is never a good time for a holiday. When the markets are great, traders want to stay and trade them; and when the markets are not so good, or the trader is having a tough time, they want to stay because they don't want to miss out on any possible opportunity to make money, and they often feel that taking a holiday when you have been losing money is somehow improper.

The question here is simple. By staying in the state that you are in now, with even further declines in energy and enthusiasm on the way, and ever lower concentration levels, are you likely to be able to trade to anywhere near your peak? In other words, is staying really going to be productive, or do you just feel you should?

After much talking, and going through with him the 'science' of oscillation, and the need for recovery to achieve peak performance, he eventually agreed to keep his holiday commitments. He then asked me what I thought about him taking his laptop so he could trade remotely while he was away! We had further discussions and eventually he committed to a three-week total rest and time away from all trading with the family.

On his return from holiday he was able to approach the markets with a fresh perspective. He really wanted to come in and trade each day, and was possessed of much greater energy and focus. He started September in a whole different mental, emotional and physical place; and as a result he was able to break out of his slump and return to profitable trading.

When you are tired and run down, and this continues day after day, it is unlikely that anything other than taking a rest is going to dramatically help you to improve your performance levels.

From a sports perspective, athletes often have breaks and rests from training to not only allow the body to rest and recover but also for mental renewal – to stop them from getting stale. How much more necessary is this in trading, then, where the contest itself is mental rather than physical!

Downtime for a Longer Long-Term

Everyone in all walks of life needs to get some downtime. People in high pressure, results-driven environments like trading definitely need to.

Whether this is making sure that you get some time to relax over the weekend, take some long weekends or plan a quarterly holiday, getting this regular recovery is a key factor not just in enabling your short-term performance to stay at peak levels, but even more so to maintaining long-term health and enabling you to stay in the markets for the long run.

Burning out – working excessively long hours in stressful environments non-stop until the point whereby only exhaustion and illness are achieved, and the person can no longer carry on – is not desirable for anyone. For the trader it reduces the longevity of their trading career, and that has an impact on their earning potential. And for an employer it means a greater turnover of staff, and that more money has to be spent on training and recruiting, as against retaining, which is by far a more effective business approach.

Life Outside of Trading

"If trading is your life, it is a torturous kind of excitement. But if you are keeping your life in balance, then it is fun. All successful traders that I have seen that lasted in the business sooner or later got to that point. They have a balanced life; they have fun outside of trading. You can't sustain it if you don't have some other focus. Eventually, you wind up overtrading or getting excessively disturbed about temporary failures."

– Michael Marcus, in *Market Wizards*

Is there life outside of trading for you?

What is that life?

How do you spend your time outside of trading?

What role do you play apart from being a trader? Parent, friend, athlete, artist?

Trading is a fantastic career. It is not only challenging, interesting and enjoyable, but it can also offer the opportunity to live a fantastic lifestyle. It is time, if you haven't already, to build in a good balance by incorporating things from such a lifestyle into your own life. Active interests, and emotional investments outside of trading, are critical for trading! You have an enviable capacity for involving yourself in some amazing things; and they will only help you become a high-performance trader more swiftly.

Practical Strategy: Enhancing Balance and Lifestyle

Firstly, assess where you are at in terms of your overall trading development, as this will help to clarify what your key focus is as a trader. And secondly, assess your life situation – where are you at personally.

Taking regular breaks away from trading is very important to keep you fresh and focussed, to prevent excessive fatigue and burnout, and to keep your perspectives on the market and on trading in general. How will you ensure that you get your required level of breaks/recovery periods/holidays?

Having a balanced lifestyle does have many benefits for traders. How do you currently achieve that balance? Are there ways in which you could achieve greater balance? What do you enjoy doing that you could do more of?

STRATEGY 31

Plan Your Growth

"One of the key factors behind the success of the traders at Schneider Trading is the planned growth that we put in place for them. We help them to grow into their P&L in a controllled way through the strategic allocation of their trading limits."

– Matthew Silvester, head of training, Schneider Trading Associates

Competence, Then Size

As a trader progresses along their career, one of the obvious development and growth areas is the *size* of their trading – the number of contracts, shares or pounds per point that the trader trades in their positions. Most traders I have worked with look at increasing size as a key performance measure, and (I would have to say) as a key bragging right!

The important thing with increasing size, though, is to make sure that you are using it as a growth factor on top of your improving trading performance capabilities, and not instead of such progress. What I mean by that is that some traders look to use size as a P&L accelerator – to make more money per trade. Trading size will of course have an impact on P&L. But it is important to let increasing size work alongside or slightly lag behind growth and development in skills, knowledge, attitudes and behaviours; or obvious disaster can follow.

Where traders aggressively increase size at the expense of developing competencies, a backlash to this at some point in the future becomes inevitable; and because they have increased their stake, the damage is proportionately greater. Traders should focus on developing their trading competence, establishing high-performance trading behaviours – and then, once the gains from working on these begin to bed down, size at last becomes a safe and significant P&L enhancer.

Practical Strategy: Increasing Size – the 4 Rs

1. Reasons

Why do you want to increase your trading size? For example, sometimes it might be off the back of having had a good trading day (or couple of days); sometimes because you feel you should, as you haven't increased your size for a while; sometimes because your head of desk/trader manager suggests it. The key factor, for me, is that size should only be increased as part of a planned and considered approach – the reason should be developmental and not financial!

2. Readiness

Trading account – if you increased your size and you lost money what would be the impact on your account, and how would you feel about that? If you had a string of sustained losses (I use a trader's metrics to look at average statistical drawdown periods to calculate this), what would the impact be and how would you feel? The most important factor once you increase size is to be able to sustain trading it to get the positive returns alongside any losses, and not to get caught up in chopping and changing in a reactionary approach to your P&L swings.

3. Right size

Comfort, stretch, panic. The increments at which a trader increases size are very important, as once the next size increase takes a trader into the panic zone (see diagram) then their execution of the strategy will be impaired by added feelings of stress, greater worry of loss and reduced cognitive functioning. When increasing size, it is important to move from the comfort zone into stretch and *not* panic. How do you know where you are, and where you're going? This is largely intuitive, although the application of a bit of common sense is involved, too.

4. Rehearsal

Let's say you are trading four contracts and decide to double to eight. Imagine a typical loss but with eight contracts, and now imagine a string of losses with eight contracts – how does that feel? If a bit uncomfortable, then that is to be expected – if you want to throw up, then that is *feedback*! How about with six contracts? Five? Through using this process you can begin to get a feel for what trading size may be best – whenever in doubt, go for the smallest increment you can. It avoids traumatising yourself, and you'll make progress more reliably: remember the tortoise and the hare!

Increasing trading size

Your goal when increasing size is to move from the comfort zone into stretch, whilst avoiding the panic zone where your trading decisions may be adversely affected and fear lurks.

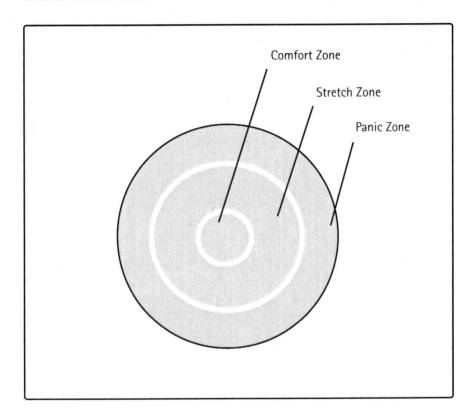

STRATEGY 32

Generate New Trading Behaviours

"Change is the law of life."

– John F. Kennedy

Performance Improvement is Behaviour Change

Becoming a better trader is a process of transformation and will involve you making changes – perhaps, for example, in the way that you think, feel or behave. Your trading performance is a reflection of your trading behaviours; therefore performance improvement is about behaviour change.

Enabling people to change behaviour and therefore improve performance is a large part of what I do as a coach and trainer. It is not always an easy or straightforward process, as I am sure you can imagine.

The Change Process

The first point that you must consider when you are looking to initiate a change of behaviour is what the current behaviour is that you wish to change, and what the reason is for wanting to change it. I also like to ask clients if they can think of a positive intention behind the old behaviour. That is, could the behaviour have once served, or tried to serve, them in some useful way that may not be useful anymore?

Secondly, you need to have a clear idea of the new behaviour that you would like to replace the old one. If possible, it is good to see if this new behaviour can meet the positive intention of the old behaviour as well. Being specific is also very important.

Exercise: Letting Go of the Old Behaviour and Deciding on the New Behaviour

The old behaviour that I choose to release and let go of is...

The positive intention behind the behaviour has been...

I choose to let go of this behaviour now because...

The new behaviour that I will adopt is...

This new behaviour will help me by...

I am committed to making this behaviour change because...

Knowing the behaviour you want to change, and the one that you would like, is not enough on its own. You need to be able to create some motivation to actually *make* the change! Behavioural change is not a passive process that just occurs with the wave of a magic wand – it requires sustained energy and focus and they need to be fuelled by motivation!

One factor that can be important in generating behaviour change is how much the person really wants to change.

How important is it for you to make that change now? You can generate motivation and a desire to change by creating some leverage.

Exercise: Creating Leverage to Change

What are the costs to you if you do not make the change? List them. Read through them. Vividly imagine each one happening.

What are the benefits to you when you do make the change? List them. Read through them. Vividly imagine each one happening.

You can take this a step further by using a strategy known as the Dickens Pattern. In Dickens' *Christmas Carol*, Scrooge is only able to make changes in his behaviour once he has had the shock of seeing his potential future. I often use this strategy with clients who I feel will really need some leverage to create the changes required.

Exercise: The Dickens Pattern

First, let's look at your possible future if you were to carry on doing what you are doing already, and not make any changes.

Relax and close your eyes.

Imagine going forward in time to a point six months into the future. Imagine that you still have all of your old behaviours. What do you notice about your performance? What can you see? What can you hear? How does it feel? Really magnify any images, sounds and feelings that are negative and undesirable.

Now repeat this process but going 12 months into the future, and then again by going two to five years, and maybe even further if necessary.

Now let's look at your alternative future. Imagine that you have let go of that old behaviour now and made that change happen. You are behaving and performing as you would ideally like to.

Relax and close your eyes.

Imagine going forward in time to a point six months into the future. Imagine that you still have all of these new behaviours. What do you notice about your performance? What can you see? What can you hear? How does it feel? Really magnify the intensity of the images, sounds and feelings of doing things like this now. Notice how naturally and easily you are performing and how great it feels.

Now repeat this process but going 12 months into the future, and then again by going two to five years and maybe even further if necessary.

At the end of the process ask yourself, "Which future would I like to create for myself?"

Will Power is Not Always Enough

In his book *Change or Die*, Alan Deutschman investigates why even despite having strong reasons to change – e.g. cardiac patients who are told that unless they change their lifestyle habits, they will have a repeat heart attack and likely die – people do not always do so. He looked at many different environments where change programmes were in place, and he noted that, of those that were most effective, the following components were evident:

Relate

You form a new emotional relationship with a person or community that inspires and sustains hope.

Repeat

The new relationship helps you to learn, practise and master the new habits and skills that you need. It takes a lot of repetition over time before new patterns of behaviour become automatic and seem natural; until you act in the new way without thinking about it. This is the training phase.

Reframe

The new relationship helps you to learn new ways of thinking about your situation and your life.

Relate

You want to find a person or a group of people who can support you in your behaviour change process. This could be a coach, a mentor, a colleague, a good friend or a family member. It has to be someone who really believes that you can make the change and will keep you motivated, and on track, right up until when the change has become permanent.

Repeat

You need to decide upon a plan of action as to how you will train and condition yourself to make the behaviour change. It will likely include physically performing the behaviour, supported by some psychological strategies such as those from this chapter and also throughout the book (see STRATEGIES 19, 21, 23).

Reframe

How can you see your situation differently? Reframing is a powerful skill to have, and you can start to change perspective by using a wide lens or long lens view, as discussed in STRATEGY 28 on toughness.

I remember hearing about a golf psychology coach who told his clients that they would have to practise the techniques hundreds of times before they became ingrained and automatic and they really began to benefit from them. This takes commitment, energy and time.

If you are going to work at developing a new behaviour, then do so with realistic expectations of what it will take. It is natural to experience a drop off in motivation after a while – at this point stop, reflect, renew your leverage and go again! It is often quoted that changing a habit takes between 21 and 28 days – factors such as what the habit is, how ingrained it is, the frequency and magnitude of the effects of the habit, the person's willingness to change, and so on, will all influence this. However, for simplicity, let's assume that with 21-28 days of focussed conditioning, you can change a habit, and reprogramme a behaviour.

What I would add to that is that it takes something approaching 90 days to really ingrain it and to begin to receive its benefits in full.

Doing Things Differently

In developing your trading skills and abilities you are essentially going through a period of conditioning. For some part of that process you will be conditioning new skills from scratch, whilst for others you may have to re-condition yourself, to overcome old habits and ways of doing things.

It's all in the mind

Every action, feeling and behaviour that you have is the result of the activation of a neural pathway in the brain. A neural pathway is a connection or series of connections between the neurons in the brain. Essentially each pathway is the mental pattern for the skill, feeling or behaviour. These neural pathways are created and then developed and strengthened through practice and repetition; and after time they will become automatic – habitual.

Exercise: New Behaviour Generator

Generating new behaviours can come consciously, through willpower, but can also be assisted and accelerated through utilising your unconscious – where most of your habits and automatic behaviours are actually stored. To enable you to utilise unconscious programming of your behaviours and to ingrain the neural pathways required for your brain to trigger and perform those behaviours, utilising visualisation is, in my opinion, a very powerful technique.

Here is a visualisation for behaviour change – a New Behaviour Generator.

The New Behaviour Generator is a visualisation technique. You may find it easier to do if you record it and then listen to it or ask a friend or colleague to read it to you. If you're uncomfortable, as with any of the other similar techniques in this book, it is okay to pass.

Make yourself comfortable, close your eyes. Take a moment to relax, perhaps by focussing on your breathing, really noticing how each time you breathe out you can relax even more.

Think about and identify the desired behaviour you want for yourself.

Imagine sitting in a cinema with a large screen in front of you. On that screen notice a movie running of you with your new desired behaviour. Notice what you do, how you look, how you move/sit/stand, what you say and how you say it, how you feel.

Decide whether you are happy with this new behaviour and really want to programme and install it.

If not, make the changes you need to and start again.

If you are happy then run the movie again but this time step inside the screen, imagining yourself there now looking out through your own eyes. Notice what you can see; what you can hear; how it feels to do things like this now. Really pay attention to how you perform with your new behaviours now and notice how easily and naturally things come. Make any further refinements that you need to.

N.B. If you need to, make sure that you adjust any negative references or slip back to old behaviours – ONLY PROGRAMME YOUR DESIRED BEHAVIOUR!

Ask yourself what it's like to do things with your new behaviour(s).

Imagine a future situation where you want to behave that way. See, hear and feel everything as you imagine yourself performing well at that point in the future now.

Open your eyes and return to the present moment.

Imagine that you are the new you with the desired behaviours. This is called 'Acting As If' and is a powerful strategy on its own. Get up and walk around as that new person. Notice how it feels.

If the feeling is strong then you may wish to consider creating an anchor/trigger for that feeling by making a fist or some other subtle but distinctive gesture.

Begin using the new behaviour as soon as possible.

STRATEGY 33

Utilise Your Strengths and Successes

"Learn to love your losses, but love learning from your profits."

– Shaun Downey

Success and Failure Leave Clues

I remember working with a young and very talented bond trader who felt that he was trading quite well, but that his results were not reflective of that. I had him do some analysis of his trading, and we went through his trade logs to assess where he was making money and where he was typically losing money, to see if there were any patterns.

The trader was able to identify that a significant proportion of his losses came between 1030-1100 and 1230, and that his most consistent and most profitable period was between 0800-1000 and 1300-1600. When we looked into this further he discovered that he traded well off the open in the morning, and traded well around the afternoon session when the US entered the market. Where he was losing his money was in the "scrap", as he called it, after 1030. This was a time when, in his perception, the only people still trading were the people who had lost money off the open, who wanted to get it back; and he never traded this period well. The trading during this period was very scrappy and the volumes were often lower.

This had an effect on his mindset and also on his execution, both of which were factors in his larger percentage of losing trades during this period. Going through this process and analysing when he was trading well, and identifying where he was utilising his strengths best, enabled him to make a significant increase in his profitability. He also used that time from 1030-1230 to go to the gym and to eat his lunch, thus achieving greater balance and recovery, higher energy, less losses and more profits!

Are You Utilising Your Strengths and Successes?

Typically, most traders who come to 1:1 coaching come because they feel that they are having a tough time and are underperforming – this is about 80% of traders. The other 20% come because they are doing well, but would like to be doing better – they want to improve their performance, learn more, develop themselves to get them as close to achieving their potential as possible. In all coaching situations, one of the questions that I ask is:

"What are your strengths as a trader?"

It can take some traders quite a long time to really begin to list their strengths. Have a go yourself.

Exercise: Identifying Strengths

Make a list of your strengths as a trader:

How did you get on?

It is important to understand what your strengths are as a trader. Regardless of whether you are looking to get out of a tough time, or to move onwards to new levels of performance, one of the tools that you have at your disposal in both situations is your strengths.

To begin to be able to use these we must then consider a secondary question:

"How do you utilise your strengths to maximise your trading potential?"

Exercise: Strength Utilisation

How do you currently utilise your strengths within your trading?

How could you utilise them more effectively?

(contd.)

This is important because it can help you to understand how well you are utilising a powerful resource that you already have. Of course, with this it is also important to think about ways in which you may be able to utilise your strengths even more fully or effectively.

Real Life Example

Sean was a trader who was very talented and embraced risk! When he was trading well he was unstoppable and generated phenomenal P&L. However, when he was off form, his losses and drawdown periods were also huge. I remember doing some analysis with Sean, again looking at where he tended to make money and where he tended to lose money; where he traded well and where he traded not so well.

As we went through this process, it soon became very clear that Sean had an extraordinary talent for trading around economic releases, speeches and events, and that he had a very high success rate and P&L return from his strategy in these areas. Where he tended to lose a lot of money was in trading intraday in markets that were not moving much.

After we had completed this analysis, the pattern and the strategy to follow were pretty clear, and Sean was able to adopt a new approach to his trading based on playing to his strengths. He utilised bigger positions for his core economic-release based strategy, and because he still wanted to trade intraday he did so – but reduced his trading positions to a significantly smaller amount, to mitigate his risk.

Other Perspectives, and Strength to Strength

You could also, if possible, ask other people who know you as a trader for feedback as to your strengths. Colleagues, trader managers, coaches/trainers, should all be able to help you ascertain what they *really* are. You will never be able to work them all out alone.

It is also important to recognise that your strengths will be *contextual*, and that a strength in one area may be a weakness elsewhere; and furthermore that, over time, strengths may actually become overused and become a weakness as environments and you change and evolve. Identifying a strength's fundamental nature, and evaluating it regularly, is therefore also important – especially if you are in the midst of a challenging time.

Of course, just playing to your strengths does not mean that we shouldn't also look at other areas for improvement, but in my experience there is perhaps a tendency from most traders to over obsess with their weaknesses and to underplay and fail to utilise their strengths and abilities. You have to look at performance overall.

- Can I raise my performance level by focussing on and utilising my strengths more effectively?

- Can I raise my performance level by developing my weaknesses(s)?

STRATEGY 34

Mind Your Language

"Your performance is profoundly influenced by your thoughts –
by the things you imagine and you say to yourself."

– Jeffrey Hodges, *Champion Thoughts Champion Feelings*

Your Thoughts Are Powerful

Your thoughts are powerful – they make things happen. They are the building blocks of your beliefs, attitudes, behaviours and crucially your self-image; and they also affect you physically, as we know from polygraphs (lie detectors). But few people really seem to understand the impact and importance of their thinking. Part of becoming a high performer in any field means taking control of your thoughts.

Pretty much everyone seems to know that you are supposed to think positively, yet how many of us actually do this?

"Research suggests that the average person talks to themselves about 50,000-60,000 times per day, and most of that is about themselves; of which it is suggested by psychologists that approximately 80% of this may be negative."

– Jack Canfield, *The Success Principles*

Imagine the impact of this. These positive thoughts can be referred to as PETs – performance-enhancing thoughts; whilst the negative ones are known as PITs – performance-interfering thoughts. Examples of PETs might include, "This is a good challenge"; "Be patient and you will profit". Whilst PITs might include, "This market is just out to get me"; "I can't do this".

Developing your ability to monitor your thoughts, to direct them towards the positive and to catch and discourage negative thinking, is a key. For most of us, a large proportion of our thinking has become automatic – habitual – and so we feel that our thoughts just happen to us. You need to realise the obvious: that you think your thoughts – that they are the product of you and that you must take responsibility for them, before you can start to control them. Control of your thoughts begins with making a decision to do so!

Exercise: Thought Awareness

This exercise will help you to raise your awareness of your thinking.

Keep a thoughts journal by your trading desk. Throughout the day make a note of your thoughts as you notice them. Keep two lists. One for PETs and one for PITs. It can be really useful to make a note of the thought, the time and the situation.

At the end of the week, review your journal. How was the quality of your thinking? What was the balance between PETs and PITs? Did you have any specific thoughts that seemed to recur? Were there any particular situations that triggered particular thoughts?

From Critic to Coach

Once you have developed an awareness of your thinking, the next stage is to take some control of your thoughts – to proactively choose only the best thoughts for yourself, and to also get into the habit of recognising negative thoughts and replacing them with more useful or positive ones. This process is often referred to as thought-stopping.

When we are thinking negatively it is often that we are being very self-critical and this is the voice of our inner critic. The inner critic can serve us well by providing useful feedback, but the critical style in which it is delivered is often not that useful. What you want to do instead is to utilise the feedback but transform the delivery of the message – imagine having your own coach, someone who really knows you well and wants you to succeed, who is a great communicator and who has the skill to deliver powerful messages in a very positive way. We want to transform our inner critic into that inner coach.

Exercise: Thought-Stopping and Replacing, Negative into Positive

Identify: Tune in to your thoughts – scan them for positive, negative, neutral.

Stop: When you identify a negative thought, coming from the critic, you want to have a process to stop it, e.g. say, "STOP!" or perhaps imagine an image of a red traffic light, or the sound of a referee's whistle.

Replace: Replace your negative thought with a more positive one. What would the coach say?

Doing this is a skill that takes time. It is often known as reframing. One way that you can help yourself is to identify all of the typical situations when you encounter negative thinking, list those thoughts and then alongside each one write down a thought that you could use in the same situation that would be more useful/positive. Mentally rehearse being in those situations, but now hear yourself using your new positive thoughts instead – do this enough times and you will find that over time they will naturally pop into your head in those situations.

Negative	Positive
Why did I let that trade run past my stop!	What can I learn from that which will make me a better trader?
Don't mess up again!	Relax, focus and execute the trade.
This market is out to get me today.	The market is the market and doesn't even know I am here. Focus on trading my strategy.
This market is too quiet to make any money. I will have to trade soon.	I can make money and I will make money as long as I keep focussed and let the trades come to me.
Everyone else seems to be so much better than me.	Everyone is different. Stay focussed on my performance and my progress.
Trading is too difficult and stressful.	Trading is challenging. The adversity makes me stronger and better.

Exercise: Choose Positive Language – Performance Cues

Performance cues are a technique used to enhance performance through directing your thoughts and, therefore, your behaviour. They are positive words or brief statements that confirm and support the achievement of an objective or a goal. Performance cues are a way in which you can choose what you specifically want to think in particular situations.

Writing Performance Cues

Think about specific trading situations within your day, and reflect on the language you use. Think about a word or phrase that you could use to prompt and drive you in the direction of your desired behaviours. If you are aware that you are using any negative commands, or telling

> **" Use positive words or statements that confirm and support the achievement of an objective or goal. "**

yourself what not to do, then find an alternative way of giving yourself this information in a positive way – write a performance cue and start using this instead.

Make sure your performance cues are effective by ensuring that you follow the three points below:

1. Performance-focussed – ensure that your cue links in what you want to achieve

2. Positive – what you do want, NOT what you are trying to avoid

3. Short and simple – a word or a brief phrase; keep them short and punchy as you want to be able to use them quickly, but also not let them start to get in the way of your performance.

STRATEGY 35

Be Persistent!

"Never, never, never give up."

– Sir Winston Churchill

You Could be One Trade, One Day, One Week or One Month Away from Success

"Without doubt the one thing that I would tell the beginning trader is to never give up. Never, never, never! This business of trading has so much to give once it is mastered. Trading is simple but it is not easy. It offers incredible freedom accompanied by monetary rewards. There is an old Chinese adage that states, "the smart man learns from his mistakes but the wise man learned from the mistakes of others". I succeeded because I never gave up! In fact, even when times were bad I knew that success was around the corner. However, there were a lot of corners almost like a never ending circle before I reach the promised land."

– Larry Pasavento, hedge fund manager

In my days as a sports performance coach providing psychological support to athletes, I spent a lot of time working with junior swimmers and I noticed something really interesting.

At about the age of 13 or 14, male junior swimmers vary in physical size enormously as they are all growing and going through adolescence at different rates. The line-up for an event can sometimes look like you have 11-18 year olds all in the same race. The first thing I noticed was that the swimmers who were bigger and more powerful at this stage had a tendency to rely on their power to win them races, and in some cases where there were swimmers who also had real talent they would rely on this too. But generally the outcome of this would be that these swimmers would not always work as hard as the other smaller swimmers in training – indeed they would often not even turn up!

Over time, and towards the ages of 16-18, the size and physical nature of the swimmers began to even out. The swimmers who had once been the smaller and least powerfully built now had the size, the technique, the conditioning and the *work ethic*; whereas the formerly bigger swimmers now had just the size and whatever level of natural talent they possessed. Accidental and temporary advantage had bred complacency and incompetence.

As the swimmers raised their performance levels and started to break through to national level, the standard in training and racing was much higher – and unless you had the work ethic it was extremely difficult to progress. Here size and talent was not enough. Often swimmers who were strong and talented in the early stages dropped out, whilst those swimmers who were smaller in the early days, and frequently lost but *kept on keeping on*, and persevered, did significantly better.

I have seen the same phenomenon in trading. On some graduate courses, the traders who do well from the beginning, those with a natural talent perhaps, are not always the best traders at the end of the course or over time. Likewise, traders who find trading difficult to begin with can easily be put off and give up; when they ought to do the opposite.

Whether you are big and strong, naturally talented or not, the one key aspect that successful people have in common is that they persisted long enough to make it! JUST KEEP GOING! Ahead of you, every brick wall you might otherwise end up bashing your head against, is surmountable by following the advice of this book and the other traders and experts it points you to.

"Persistence is probably the single most common quality of high achievers."

– Jack Canfield, *The Success Principles*

"I have worked with people who I may have thought had little chance of making it, but they stuck at it and proved me wrong!"

– Nick McDonald, Trade With Precision

How Long Do I Have to Wait Before I Make it?

"Most people give up just when they are about to taste success."

– H. Ross Perot, American billionaire and former US presidential candidate

How long do you have to keep going for before you make it? There is no single answer to this question. It will vary from person to person, dependent on skills, abilities, the time available, openness and willingness to learn, motivation and passion; and also, to a degree, on a little good fortune in terms of market conditions and events. It also depends on how you are defining 'making it'. But, by having followed the strategies in this book, you will have given yourself the strongest chance of it happening *sooner* rather than later.

Practical Strategy: Being Persistent

- Understand that becoming an expert trader takes years, and set your goals and targets accordingly with a realistic approach.

- Focus on your own performance and progress, and not that of others who may be ahead of or behind you on the learning curve. Every individual trader brings unique skills, abilities and attitudes to the table and will progress at their own rate.

- Establish compelling goals and strong motivations to provide you with the direction and fuel to keep you going (STRATEGY 3).

- Develop resilience (STRATEGY 28).

"This is no easy business, do not expect easy riches. You will need to work for success. Markets will frustrate you, test you, try to beat you. Do not let them win."

– SJG, trader